ON WINGS OF
MOURNING

ON WINGS OF MOURNING

Our Journey
through
Grief and Recovery

Carol A. and William J.
Rowley

WORD BOOKS
PUBLISHER
WACO, TEXAS

A DIVISION OF
WORD, INCORPORATED

ON WINGS OF MOURNING: OUR JOURNEY THROUGH GRIEF AND RECOVERY

Scripture quotations in this publication are from the following sources:
The King James Version of the Bible (KJV).
The New International Version of the Bible (NIV), published by the Zondervan Corporation, copyright © 1978 by the New International Bible Society.
The Living Bible, Paraphrased (TLB), copyright © 1971 by Tyndale House Publishers, Wheaton, Illinois.

Library of Congress Cataloging in Publication Data

Rowley, Carol A., 1941–
  On wings of mourning.

  Bibliography: p.
  1. Bereavement—Religious aspects—Christianity.
2. Consolation. 3. Children—Death—Religious aspects—
Christianity. 4. Rowley, Carol A., 1941–   .
5. Rowley, William J., 1941–   . I. Rowley, William J.,
1941–   . II. Title.
BV4907.R68   1984   248.8'6   84–7263
ISBN 0–8499–0390–4

To our children
DEVON and DANIEL
who have taught us the
meaning of love
one through her death and
the other through his life

Contents

Acknowledgments

We wish to express our appreciation to three significant people at Word Books: to Al Bryant who first encouraged Carol to complete the story of Devon; to Ernie Owen who has treated us as people of value; and to Beverly Phillips who has skillfully worked to make our story understandable to its readers.

We would also like to express our thankfulness to all of our friends and family mentioned in these pages who let us know of their love for us during a difficult period of our lives.

Preface

This is a story of hope. Sadness is contained within its pages, but the real story is that of the human spirit's capacity to heal, to overcome, to triumph. It is a story for everyone. Perhaps you have lost a child or significant loved one. Reading our story may help you during your own period of recovery. Maybe you have friends who have had a similar experience. If so, you will understand better their ordeal and know how to comfort them. It may be that no one in your life has recently died, but you are nevertheless experiencing the loss of someone or something from your life that is of great value to you. Our hope is that you will learn, as we did, that it is possible to find something of great value as a consequence of your loss.

The story you are about to read is but one context in which loss and recovery are experienced. You, of course, have your own history and can supply your own context in which to grow. But the insight we can all gain is that it is possible to translate utter tragedy into a higher level of personal growth and maturity.

When we began to write the story of Devon, a friend of ours asked us why we thought our experience was unique enough to write about. We are not sure that it is, but we hope our response to our experience is significant enough to help and comfort others who may be making their own journey through grief and recovery.

A brief word regarding the format of the book is in order before you begin. Carol is a librarian by profession, and therefore a storyteller. Bill is a counseling professional, and therefore a therapist. There are books on grief and death written by other parents, and there are also books on the topic written by counseling professionals who have not personally overcome such an experience. This book is an attempt to combine the two: a story by parents and a counseling professional. Carol tells the story of Devon, and Bill addresses and explores the various issues as a therapist and father.

You have two options for reading this book. The first option is to read the book as we have presented it—reading each chapter in order. The second is to read Devon's story without interruption. To do this, read the odd-numbered chapters first. Then, for a professional's view of the process of grief and recovery, read all the even-numbered chapters. Then finish by reading the epilogue.

Writing this book in many ways is the culmination of our own recovery and growth. It is our hope that it will contribute to the healing of others as well.

Carol and Bill Rowley
La Mesa, California

Part One

THE BEGINNING

An Ill Wind

*T*he sound of the telephone tore through the quiet page of a Sunday morning. I knew even before I picked up the phone who the caller would be and the content of the message: "Devon is . . . Devon Rowley's condition is worsening rapidly. You need to get here as soon as possible."

My chest felt a sudden pressure, as though the hot August day had suddenly intensified in humidity. It was the pediatric ward of the hospital calling. It meant that our thirteen-month-old daughter had minutes to live. There was no sense of panic as we hurriedly dressed, only a strong sense of purpose to make it in time. After all, we had experienced many terror-filled moments during the past five months. It had become the norm. Trauma turned my husband and me into efficient machines, capable of operating on the outside with an absence of feeling on the inside.

My husband backed the car out quickly. I found myself reviewing the past five months as we sped toward the hospital. At what moment had life stopped being normal? What had delayed the miracle we had expected in our daughter's behalf? Where was God when we needed Him?

It had all begun about twenty minutes of five on the Monday afternoon before Easter of 1977. I was making my way blindly through traffic, tears flowing down my face, on my way to a previously unscheduled appointment with the head of the hospital's pediatric department. A few moments before I had listened with disbelief as a pediatric nurse specialist had said, "Your baby appears to have a large mass on the right side of her abdomen. It is imperative that you take her to see a doctor at the Kaiser Hospital this afternoon."

As I fought my way through the rush hour traffic, my mind tried to deal with what I had just heard. My eight-year-old son, Danny, sat in the back seat of the car, listening to my torrent of angry words, while my baby daughter played quietly in her car seat, unaware of the drama soon to unfold around her.

How could a mere nurse without any authority from a doctor make such a serious health statement? Where was the careful shielding of the vulnerable patient or patient's family that I had witnessed on medical television programs or read about? How could this beautiful child have anything that seriously wrong with her without showing severe symptoms?

As the three of us hurried into the doctor's waiting room, I was both relieved and alarmed to find my husband, Bill, waiting for us. It must be something serious for them to have contacted him to meet us here. We were ushered in to see the doctor, and as his practiced hands examined Devon she screamed her loudest at the indignity of two examinations in one day.

The doctor's first response was that he could not determine a mass but perhaps the liver was enlarged. He suggested that we return the following day for a series of tests that would give us a definite picture of her problem.

That evening as I put Devon to bed, while dinner guests sipped coffee in the living room, it seemed that the day had been unreal and that now while I held this dark-haired child near, I had regained reality and safety. The lullaby I often made up from the hymn came to my lips as I tiptoed from her room, "Jesus give to Devon calm and sweet repose. With Thy tenderest blessings may her eyelids close."

I phoned my mother, a retired nurse, the next day to tell her the bombshell which had been dropped into our lives. I remember her guarded responses, and the silence that followed my mentioning an enlarged liver. Her closing words before we hung up were reassuring, with a promise that she and Dad would be praying for us. I had a great deal of faith in their prayers.

By Friday we still had not received word as to the outcome of the tests we had gone through on Tuesday. When we talked to our doctor by phone, he told us that some of the tests had been sent out of the hospital and had not been returned yet. He asked us to come in Saturday morning to have Devon reexamined if the fever was still persisting. The fever continued and now I noticed her appetite had begun to dwindle.

The Saturday morning before Easter in our neighborhood has always been the traditional Easter egg hunt. The surrounding cul-de-sac yards come alive as children scramble to find eggs and parents stand around and drink coffee and chat. Since our appointment was to be at 8:00 A.M., I asked my neighbor to watch over our eight-year-old son and be sure he found at least one egg.

After examining Devon the doctor expressed concern over the continuing fever and then confided that the test results were still not available. My eyes filled with angry tears as my frustration mounted to overflowing. All week long I had dealt with the uncertainty of the situation, and having to wait longer to know the truth, good or bad, seemed too much. I excused myself and taking Devon with me told Bill I would wait for him in the car.

The doctor explained to Bill after I had left that it would probably be best to put Devon into the hospital so that the tests could be done on an inpatient basis, assuring us of results the same day.

We were given a single room on the second floor of the hospital that looked out on the roof. A kind of park scene greeted my eyes as I looked out the window that gray Saturday morning. Big wine barrels of pink and white petunias bloomed profusely. Two or three ficus trees moved quietly in an unfelt breeze. I held Devon up to see, and I talked to her about the pretty flowers in a voice less than steady. She responded as always by pointing with a pudgy finger and wrinkling up her nose as if to smell them.

Throughout the day, numerous blood samples, urine samples, and x-rays were conducted. In between the tests, I tried to pray and found only a wall of anxiety too large to pray over.

When the results came at 7:00 that evening, Bill and I were exhausted. Our doctor closed the door to Devon's room. He explained that the x-rays revealed a mass in her right kidney, probably a malignant Wilm's tumor. If the tumor was contained entirely within the kidney, it would be removed without danger to life since kidneys are paired organs. He further explained she would need to have surgery immediately, and it would be done at the Kaiser Hospital in Hollywood.

What words really express the range of emotions that enveloped us? Horror, disbelief, overwhelming fear? I am sure they were all present. I think the shock we felt cushioned us until we walked out of the hospital and into the parking lot. Then I heard Bill's whisper, "My baby . . . I don't want to lose my little girl." A quick picture flitted through my mind of him running up the stairs at home, two at a time each day after work and calling out, "Is there a little girl up here somewhere?" Then would follow his big smile as he caught her up in his arms from her bed or dressing table.

When we arrived home there were calls to be made to family and friends. Bill began the calls but found he could not complete a sentence without breaking down. I had been crying off and on all during the day and now, since my tears were all but gone, I made the calls. It was to happen again and again throughout the coming weeks. One being in control, then a reversal of roles.

It didn't seem right that Easter morning should turn out to be such a beautiful day. We hurried to get things ready to go to Hollywood, a suburb of Los Angeles. My folks were flying in from Denver to take care of Danny while Bill and I took Devon to Los Angeles. As we were eating breakfast there was a knock at the door. When I opened it, I found a pan of hot rolls waiting for me and one of my neighbors hurrying away. I called after her to thank her. She never turned around. I knew she was too overcome to speak.

Just as Bill was getting ready to leave for the airport to pick up my folks, the doorbell rang. A good friend had come by to assure us of his love. We all hugged and then struggling to maintain control, he offered a simple prayer for Devon and for us. He knew our anguish more than most because he had a little daughter, just three months younger than Devon.

Arriving a few minutes later in Devon's hospital room, I caught sight of a pink and purple crocheted basket, handmade by hospital volunteers, filled with Easter eggs. I realized that I had forgotten to hide Danny's basket last night. Families belong together. How was I going to deal with half of my family in San Diego and the other half in Los Angeles? My support system seemed to be coming apart.

2

Recognizing
the Impact of Change

Sitting in my office with a respected colleague, I was discussing a psychological issue, one that at the time seemed so significant but has long since escaped my memory. As a guidance coordinator for the San Diego County Department of Education, it was my task to serve as a consultant to counselors, psychologists, teachers, and administrators working in the school setting. Theoretically, the position made me something of a counselor's counselor, someone a professional could turn to when a question arose about psychological, emotional, or mental development. The phone rang, interrupting our animated conversation, as it did several dozen times a day. It might be an educator in a small school district requiring some kind of direct, on-site assistance. Perhaps someone in a larger district needing only advice, my viewpoint, or my experience concerning a particular problem. Instead, the phone call represented one of those moments when your life is changed forever, not because you decide to be different, but because you are forced by circumstances to view life differently.

The faceless voice on the other end of the line sounded ambivalent: trying to sound calm but at the same time attempting to persuade me to accept her message as urgent. The nurse on the line said, "Dr. Rowley, your wife has taken Devon to the Kaiser Hospital to see her doctor. You should meet her there immediately." Before I could even adjust to the unexpected nature of the call, the nurse was ending our brief conversation. I turned to my colleague and said, "I sure hope that isn't something serious." As I began to fill him in on the message of the call, the phone rang again. This time it was a pediatric nurse specialist who made no mention of the call moments before. She told me she had just examined Devon during a routine examination and had discovered a large mass in her abdomen. She had advised my wife, Carol, to go immediately to her pediatrician, and she advised that I meet her there. Although unknown to me at that moment, I very shortly would be experiencing a new set of circumstances which would demand that I confront all the assumptions and conclusions I had made about life.

Only five months earlier, I had presented a paper to a state conference of counseling professionals on the topic, "Guidance Personnel 1984: Models for the Future." Devon was just a few days shy of being three months old when the paper was shared with other professionals. It began innocently enough with the statement, "A continuing question in the counseling profession has always been, 'What should we be doing in order to meet the needs of our clients?'" As I continued to make a case for a guidance model which would meet the changing needs of clients, I shared this statement with the conferees in attendance:

> At the risk of sounding too philosophical and certainly re-peating what has often been expressed, the world in which we live continually experiences and manifests growth and development, which inevitably leads to change. This change is recognized by some of us, and at other times it passes without our notice. It is often slow in development, but *it can occur in a rapid manner*. It initially might produce little impact upon us, but *it potentially demands our attention and action*. One thing is sure: change continually occurs regardless of our recognition of it, our efforts to resist it, or our attempts to affect its direction.

I had spoken of change in a narrow, philosophical, and theoretical manner. Yet I had innocently recognized that there are times when events occur rapidly, creating a tre-mendous impact and demanding our attention. Now with two phone calls, only moments old and but a few minutes long, I was living the reality of my words.

In the case of sudden events of tragic proportions, the impact is often accompanied by a sense of helplessness, loss of control, anxiety, fear, pain, and disequilibrium. At such a time, nothing in anyone's prior training or experience can completely or adequately prepare the person for the un-folding events of tragedy. Life can never be the same, in spite of an agonizing desire to have it so.

Abraham Maslow, a highly regarded psychologist who spent a lifetime studying the healthy personality, con-cluded that we generally have a tendency toward growth and positive, healthy development. Maslow believed that as our physiological needs, security needs, love and belonging needs, and esteem needs are met, we are better able to develop our potential and understand our world. What happens, though, when a serious disruption in our life

occurs, and we are no longer able to feel as secure as we
once did?

Many of us parents tend to feel secure in the idea that
the physiological needs of our children will be met through
our nurturing and responsible parenting and that the result of our behavior will be the development of relatively
healthy children. Under normal circumstances, our view
and expectations of life are regularly and consistently affirmed. When one of our children is diagnosed as having a
life-threatening illness, however, one over which we apparently have little or no control, it becomes extremely difficult to hold on to our assumption. We are bound, then, to
experience confusion and feel as though life as we have
known it is falling apart. Many times I found myself thinking, "I can't believe this is happening."

Why do we feel as though our world is falling apart when
crises hit? Is there something wrong with us? Are we abnormal? Are we less capable than others of responding in a
healthy manner to overwhelming problems? To the contrary, such feelings and emotions are appropriate and normal. When an accident, illness, or crisis occurs which has
potentially tragic consequences, it would in fact be *abnormal*
to feel well-oriented, in control, happy, and at peace.
Disorientation and disequilibrium are natural responses
to those times when our perceptions and conclusions
about life are confronted by contrasting information and
experiences.

For example, Carol and I always believed that our children would grow up in a more-or-less healthy fashion as
long as we kept them clean, bundled them up before we
took them out in bad weather, kept them away from terribly
sick children, and provided them with a balanced diet. Is it
any wonder, then, that we experienced confusion and emotional turmoil when Devon contracted or developed a disease of life-and-death proportions? How often I thought,
This isn't supposed *to happen.*

In summary, health crises are often conveyors of change. To experience confusion and turmoil during a serious illness is a natural consequence. We can find solace, however, in the knowledge that we are responding in a manner to be expected, and we can anticipate a return to a sense of equilibrium when the crisis is past.

3

Changing Currents

*T*here is nothing like a little hope thrown out to you in the midst of a hopeless experience. Before we left the San Diego Hospital that Easter morning, hope came in wearing a hospital-green uniform, and spoke in warm, reassuring tones. As I dressed little Devon for our trip to Los Angeles, the head nurse said that she was certain we would feel much better as soon as the surgery was completed. "If someone is going to have cancer, a Wilm's tumor is one of the better forms. Devon will have an 80 percent chance of survival," she said. My mind grabbed that survival figure and never gave the 20 percent mortality rate a thought. I walked out of the hospital feeling so grateful Devon had one of the "better forms" of cancer.

We were intercepted by Bill, Danny, and my parents in

the lobby. We all hugged each other bravely. Mother commented on the dark circles below Devon's dark eyes, and Devon hid her head on my shoulder. Arriving home a few minutes later, we gathered around for prayer, and my father committed us all to the care of a loving heavenly Father. With a last hug for Danny Boy, and promises to call each evening, we were on our way to Los Angeles.

As the numbness of our situation began to wear off a bit, it was replaced by my need to set a fragmented life back together. It has always been my style to deal with a problem in a straightforward way and come up with a quick and hopefully efficient solution. As we sped toward Los Angeles, my mind was eager to fix this situation of cancer by laying out all the steps we would follow, and then be home again. We carried with us Devon's medical history, along with x-rays and copies of test results. Our doctor had called ahead to the Kaiser Hospital in Hollywood to help pave our way and to consult with the surgeon. As my mind clicked off the details, I watched Devon sleep and realized that life had handed me a situation without a solution. A deep sense of anxiety and frustration began to grow within. My world was no longer one I could control or repair. I wish I could say that I handed it to God at that point and all was well. I do remember praying anxious, frantic little prayers as I looked down at that precious child, wondering if I was being tested to see what kind of faith I had and realizing that I wasn't sure myself of either the quality or the quantity of my faith.

We entered the hospital and located the admissions office—a dark, stuffy waiting room filled with fifty people, all looking ill. We sat there for nearly an hour. Devon became increasingly uncomfortable and restless. I became increasingly impatient. Bill became asseritve at last and approached the admitting clerk.

"Our baby has a malignant tumor and really needs the comfort of a bed. Since she is only eight months old, could you admit her before these adults? I don't think she can take much more waiting."

The clerk seemed impressed and within a few minutes we were in the elevator on our way to the intensive care unit on the seventh floor of the pediatric ward.

Some day I will write a brief story on my life as experienced through the sense of smell. My family has long teased me about the capacity of such a small nose. I know that one memory will always live poignantly on in my mind—that of the first odor that greeted us as the elevator opened to the seventh floor. Rubbing alcohol, the aroma of stale food, and perhaps a trace of urine all combined to make a distinct and distasteful first impression and lasting memory.

The second impression wasn't much better. I was probably remembering the petunias in the barrels on the roof garden at the Kaiser Hosital in San Diego or perhaps the semiprivate room. Nothing could have prepared me for Room 779. It was a room which held three children's beds, two sinks and two chairs. When we walked in that afternoon, two of the beds were filled, and of course two sets of parents were standing by. We were assured by the nurse that all patients would be receiving top-priority care. At the high cost of medical care, I wondered why some of that money couldn't buy a few more chairs and a few more square feet.

I undressed Devon and tried to make her feel at home. The top part of her crib was covered with a see-through plastic material. I placed some pictures of animals in bright colors within her viewing range, and put some of her toys on the little table near her bed. The whole effect fell flat compared to her well-decorated nursery at home. Her eyes darted fearfully around and she clutched my fingers. I could feel a lump forming in my throat. A sign was hung at the foot of the crib, "DO NOT PALPATE THE ABDOMEN." It sounded ominous.

After twenty or thirty minutes a young, sandy-haired intern came to examine Devon and take her medical history. We naively told him that would be unnecessary since we had hand-carried all that information from San Diego. We learned quickly that there is very little carry over from one hospital to another, and from one doctor to another.

His questions continued in an unceasing monotone until we had covered the identical ground covered in San Diego, all of which now lay in a folder on my lap. There was an awkward moment when he finished the case history and began the examination. He boldly palpated the abdomen. Should I call attention to the sign? I hesitated and then the moment was over. I knew that if it happened again I would say something. In that moment I became Devon's mediator between the medical world and the only world she had ever known: home.

When Devon seemed to be resting again, Bill and I slipped down the hall to the elevator. As we moved past open doorways, I caught glimpses of children's pale faces and guardian parents standing by. As we passed the last door before the elevator, I noticed a little black girl about four years old. Her room was filled with toys. I realized she had taken up a somewhat permanent residence. There was a gate across the doorway, which signified some isolation. Her hair was light, thin fuzz on top, giving the appearance of a soft black halo. She was darling and her smile reached out to me as we moved past. I recognized the telltale signs. Cancer knows no color barriers.

Following a supper of tasteless food in the hospital cafeteria, we hurried back upstairs in time to feed Devon her supper. It would be the last she would have for many hours because of the many tests she would undergo.

At 8:00 A.M. Monday morning, we were introduced to the surgeon and the oncologist. Was there ever such a contrast of personalities! The surgeon exuded confidence with every word. The oncologist was a serious, quiet-spoken

man with a sadness in his eyes that mirrored what was in my
heart.

We had arrived at the hospital with a great sense of
urgency. Time was surely our enemy. Every moment the
cancer could be growing. Surely the surgery would be done
within the first or second day. We were dismayed to learn
that the surgery wouldn't take place until later in the week.
When we pressed for an earlier time, the surgeon bristled.
Were we wanting to handicap his ability to pinpoint the
mass and his effectiveness by bypassing the necessary tests?

After a goodnight kiss pressed on Devon's soft curls, we
walked out of the hospital, down a block to a low budget
motel. We had no way of knowing how many days we would
be here, so we had chosen to keep a low profile financially.
The Spartan room did nothing to lift our spirits now as we
both collapsed on the bed exhausted. I reached over to a
suitcase to find my Bible. As I flipped through the pages,
I noted certain verses underlined on previous occasions
for their meaning. None seemed to hold the extraordinary
comfort I needed at the moment.

Bill interrupted my search by saying, "I'm not sure what
God has in mind for us in all of this, but I think we should
pray with the possibility in mind that when they open her
up, they won't even find the tumor to be malignant."

We prayed and cried together. Then it was time to call
home to pass on the information and bring my folks up to
date on that day's happenings. Danny came on the phone
and spoke in one word answers to our questions. Then,
before Grandma took the phone, he had one haunting
question for us that was to be repeated almost every time we
called home in the days ahead: "When are you coming
home?"

In the days that followed Bill and I moved through a gray
world of fear, anxiety, and emotional and physical fatigue.
It seemed that the lows kept outdoing themselves. But if it
was wearing on us, what must it have been for such a young

child who had suddenly moved from a protected, loving environment to a strange world of new faces and increasing discomfort? We took turns being with her almost every hour, speaking in quiet assuring voices, loving her with our hands and eyes, and, when possible, assisting with her care.

Monday morning a scan of the liver and spleen was done. Both were found to be normal. A pyelogram and cystoscopy done the same day confirmed the presence of an intraabdominal mass, exerting pressure on her right ureter. The following day an inferior vena cavagram again confirmed the mass and further pinpointed its location for the surgeon.

Tuesday following the test results, we met with the surgeon who went over his procedure and told us the surgery was scheduled for the next morning. I know we both felt a sense of relief that it was finally reaching this moment.

That evening we received our first phone call from Ruth and Dick Halbert. They had never met us but offered their home to us. They had known my brother, who had served as a music director in their church many years before. They promised to come visit us in the hospital.

The church has often been compared to the body of Christ both in Scripture and in sermons. It is to serve and care for its members. It took on a new meaning that evening as Ruth and Dick came to meet us and Devon, and to renew their offer. As they were leaving Ruth handed me a small plastic plaque. It read, "Expect a Miracle." Ruth explained that it had previously been on two hospital doors of other critically ill children. Both had recovered. As I took it from her hand, I reasoned that the world, especially our world, was overdue for a miracle. That evening we added Room 779 to the other numbers on the plaque. For some reason, we never put it on her hospital door.

4

Confronting the
Crisis

*I*s there a world that is more mysterious, unfamiliar, and intimidating to most of us than the world of intensive care units, medical procedures, names of diagnostic tests, visiting hour restrictions, and daily hospital routine? It is as though everything we have ever known is thrown out and rendered useless the moment we enter a hospital.

The entire experience reminds me of how I felt on the first day at a new school when I was but a child. The day we admitted Devon to the hospital in Los Angeles, I felt like a little boy in a grown-up world. Even standing in Devon's room on that Easter morning, I felt that someone at any moment would tell me I shouldn't be there and would have to leave. When a nurse would come in to check on her condition, I often would leave in anticipation that I would be told that I was in the way. So many times I wanted to ask about Devon's condition, but I felt I would be reprimanded for asking such an inappropriate question.

As far back as I can remember to my boyhood days, I have always felt a sense of anxiety whenever I have had to face a new situation, a new environment, or a new set of people. Our son, Danny, seems to have inherited this family trait. I remember when he came home in the third grade all excited that he would be able to play in the school orchestra. As he discussed the possibility with his mother, he decided he would play a clarinet. As the evening wore on, he must have begun to wonder if he would be able to learn how to play his instrument. Finally, he announced that he had decided he didn't want to play in the orchestra after all. With an intuitive sense, Carol figured out that he was frightened to try something new. She handled it with sensitivity and creativity. She suggested to Danny that they visit the music store and rent a clarinet for one month. He could learn to play a tune or two and become acquainted with it. She told him that they would return the instrument to the music store at the end of the month if he still felt like he didn't want to play in the school orchestra. The minute he got the instrument home, there was no doubt but that he would be joining the orchestra.

As the years have passed, I have developed a pretty good set of skills for hiding the anxiety that comes to me when I am faced with a new situation. Deep within, however, I am still a bit frightened to be placed in unfamiliar situations. Several years ago, Carol and I felt the need to change our place of worship. It was nothing less than grueling to visit a new church each Sunday. I always dreaded that moment when the congregation would go through its ritual of identifying those worshippers who were visiting for the very first time. And, being approached after the service by a caring member of the church was no less tension producing. What should I say? How should I act? My overwhelm-

ing thought was always the same: *Let's get out of here!* I
began to wish for the day when we would find a place that
we could comfortably call our church home.

In 1973 when I was hired to serve school districts in San
Diego County as a consultant, I was given a great deal of
freedom to develop my job, my style, my contacts, and my
priorities. Recently having finished my doctorate in counseling psychology and being recruited for what sounded
like an exciting, challenging job, I went to work on my first
day with a great deal of confidence and enthusiasm. I
walked into my office with its bare walls and empty desk
and sat down. Staring at the shiny desk top and silent
telephone, the paralyzing thought gradually intruded
upon my consciousness. "I don't know what to do. I don't
know anybody, and I don't even know where to start." The
anxiety began to rise, and my confidence began to falter. At
that very moment, in one of those exquisite seconds of
perfect timing, a secretary quietly and respectfully stood at
my office door and asked, "Is there anything I can do to
help you get started?" In desperation, I asked if she knew
where the pencils were stocked. In a calm, helpful voice,
she said she would be glad to get me some office supplies.
It wasn't the most significant morning I ever spent on that
job, but the simple task of setting up my office brought a
great sense of relief. After all, I was in the process of becoming more familiar with my environment.

Feelings of anxiety that accompany the strange and mysterious world of a hospital no doubt come as the result of a
variety of factors: the unfamiliar surroundings; strangers
who are suddenly thrust into our lives; our own feelings of
inadequacy, confusion, and fear; the busy and often heavy
work load of the doctors and nurses; and the discomfort
that some of the medical professionals feel when talking to
patients or the patient's family when they themselves are
not exactly in control of a life-threatening illness. Whatever
the cause, it all comes down to a desperate need for the

ordeal to be over as quickly as possible and for life to return to some semblance of order, control, and normalcy.

It is important to recognize, however, that it is rarely possible to hurry the pace of the healing process. Most people realize that serious physical trauma requires a lengthy recovery period. Additionally, psychologists have known for years that emotions have several key characteristics which make it difficult to overcome them rapidly. Robert Silverman in his book entitled *Psychology* notes that emotions, for example, are diffuse, persistent, and cumulative. Intense emotion is literally felt all over due to the fact that an emotional state creates an impact on the smooth muscle system, which is located throughout the entire body. Because of this diffusion, we can be left physically exhausted following emotional trauma. An intense emotional response, therefore, is much more difficult to overcome.

Silverman further explains that emotions are so persistent that they often endure long after the precipitating event has disappeared. Recently, one of my clients told me that she had had a conversation with her boyfriend that upset her terribly. She couldn't understand why she still felt anxious even though several days had passed since the argument. The answer is relatively simple: intense emotions are persistent.

The fact that emotions are cumulative means that if we begin the day with an emotional set of anxiety, we are very likely to approach the various problems and decisions of the entire day with anxiety even when anxiety may be unwarranted. This is why we can sit in a hospital room when all appears to be going well and feel an anxious knot deep in our stomachs.

It certainly is understandable why we have an intense wish for a crisis to be concluded quickly, but obviously that wish is often impossible to grant due to the nature of our physiological and emotional makeup. Almost daily Carol and I met parents in the hospital with but one wish: "I hope the doctor lets us go home soon."

In the midst of unfamiliar, anxiety-producing circumstances, we can feel more comfortable by fully appreciating the nature of how our emotions express themselves. They are actually a marvelous alarm system that alerts us to the need to release energy and to take the necessary action required when danger is imminently near. Our emotions, yes, the anxious ones, serve as the motivating factor to help us confront courageously the difficult tasks that may be ahead of us.

5

Unexpected Turbulence

As we made ourselves comfortable in the well-worn lounge on the seventh floor at eight o'clock that Wednesday morning, the elevator door opened and around the corner came Pat and Poli Petridis. Pat was Bill's sister, who lived in nearby Glendora. She and her husband sat down with us to wait out the anxious moments. I don't recall much of what was said, although we visited for more than four hours. I do remember the quiet comfort they gave us. The main thing was that they had come to share the anxiety.

The assistant surgeon met us immediately following the surgery. He told us that Devon had come through the surgery successfully and was now in the recovery room. An hour or so later the surgeon came up to give us the news. He said the right kidney had been very enlarged with a mass and had been removed. There did not appear to be any intrusion of disease into the abdominal cavity. It had definitely been cancer. The lab report would determine the course of action from here on out. I will never forget his last flippant words:

"Mother," he said, turning to me, "that little girl will live to be eighty!" It was as if he had taken care of it himself, and that was that.

It was hard to share his optimism later when that little figure was brought back up from surgery, with tubes and needles attached all over her body. Her long lashes rested quietly on her pale cheeks. I wished I could take her place. How many times I was to wish that in the days ahead.

The days passed slowly. The routine by the end of the week was to spend the better part of the day with Devon, assisting in her care as we could, eating meals nearby, and then checking on her again in the evening. We began to establish goals such as when there is no more blood in the fluid, the tube may be removed. We will pray for that. Try to keep the nurses from putting the i.v. in her scalp as it is so painful for Devon. Find out all we can from the oncologist about the various plans of treatment, and make a decision based on the best information from the doctors, and one that seems reasonable for Devon.

One evening we returned to find a nurse we had nicknamed "Peach Blossom" for her lovely peaches and cream complexion packing Devon in ice cubes. Devon's fever had risen suddenly. And now she was screaming and shivering. It was more than I could stand. What other torture awaited this poor child? I made my way blindly down the hall to the small women's room. Slamming the door, the sobs tumbled out along with thoughts like *Enough!* I didn't think it was possible to stand anymore. As I looked into the mirror, the face staring back seemed drained and older than the thirty-six years I knew it was. All the crying did nothing to assuage the bottomless pit of frustration. All my intuitions as a mother told me to take my child and get out. She was being hurt. She needed comfort. She needed to be held, but I couldn't even pick her up to hold her because of all the tubes and needles.

That weekend my folks and Danny came to Los Angeles. For a few hours we were a family once again. Danny seemed much too self-contained for an eight-year-old. He seemed to hold himself a little aloof at first. His face lit up when we talked about going to eat hamburgers. No doubt about it the way to a child's heart is through his stomach. Halfway through the meal, he seemed his old self again. His world had been full of adjustments during the past few days. But he was a survivor like the rest of us, and for the moment difficulties were forgotten in a mouthful of French fries.

The oncologist met with us early in the week to give us the laboratory report. Perhaps because of the glib statement by the surgeon, perhaps because we were still unable to face the horror of cancer, it came as a terrible blow that the tumor removed along with Devon's kidney was a grade three. This meant that some invasion into the surrounding blood vessels had occurred. Our faith was able to handle the fact that God could take care of a grade one or a grade two tumor. Both required only chemotherapy. But a grade three meant that both chemotherapy and radiotherapy would be the course of treatment, and chances of survival went down from 80 percent to 60 percent.

I made another trip to the women's room to sob and cry alone, and pray frantically to a God who had always worked difficult times out for us before. Later that day when we shared our grim news with my parents, my dad said, "You know, I am sure a cold and cancer are on equal ground as far as the power of God is concerned." The various grades of tumors were nothing to God. Devon was in His care, as were we all. But anxiety was a cold hard lump in my throat that was never really very far away. My head thought all the right kind of thoughts, but my heart was another matter.

Devon's chemotherapy was begun the day after surgery. The drug Vincristine was administered through her i.v. We waited through the first day for some adverse affects, but there were none. We felt hopeful that perhaps she would be an exception to the sickness that most always accompanies any chemotherapy. She continued to show no signs of illness, other than a dry mouth, and a strange odor to her urine.

We found that the next step, meeting the radiologist, had been arranged for the following day. We welcomed the visit to discuss our apprehension of radiotherapy with such a young child. We knew it could mean lack of development for the radiated area, perhaps even making her a cripple. Perhaps, we reasoned, it would be worse than the disease it sought to destroy. By now Devon had been freed from her i.v. and could be held. It was a freedom that we both enjoyed. Pale though she was, she was still so beautiful with dark eyes and curly dark hair. The nurses commented on her beauty, and it seemed to make her shy, as if she understood. She hid her face on my shoulder.

Devon twisted and turned on my lap as we sat down in the radiotherapy office. After introducing ourselves, Bill posed the question of whether radiotherapy would be a problem for Devon's later development. Would it cause crippling? In a manner that could only be described as direct and insensitive, the doctor replied, "This is not a question of whether or not the child might be crippled as an aftereffect of the treatment. The real question is whether or not you want this child to live! I have seen the tumor under the microscope. It was nasty. There is no way the proper course of treatment could negate radiotherapy."

With dark eyes flashing, he waited for a response. Here was a no doubt competent man, who day after day dealt out to unfortunate cancer victims the prescription of radiation.

Perhaps in facing so much human suffering, he had taken on a harsh, aloof exterior. I wondered as I looked at him, how he would react if such a child were his own. Perhaps he did not appreciate someone's questioning his judgment.

Bill thanked him for his time, and said we would be getting back to him with our answer. As we rode back up in the elevator with Devon to the seventh floor, Bill explained his next course of action. He would call our friend Cal, a psychiatrist in San Diego, and have him recommend a radiologist from whom we could get a second opinion.

The following day, the radiologist from San Diego consulted by phone with the oncologist and the laboratory, and politely told Bill that there really was no choice in the matter. Without radiotherapy, there was little chance Devon would survive. Since the second opinion agreed with the first, we concurred. The radiotherapy period was to take place in June for a period of four weeks.

When we rounded the corner the following morning from the elevator, we found Devon sitting in a highchair eating her breakfast. What a welcome sight! She seemed to be enjoying a little freedom from her bed, and she was eating well. We realized she would be moving out of intensive care within a day or so and shared the news with the other parents with children in the same room.

There were Manuel's parents, who had brought their seven-year-old son to the hospital after a car accident. Although there had not seemd to be any injury, other than a mild concussion, Manuel had begun having seizures, so had been brought into the intensive care unit for observation. Everyone Manuel knew brought him large and small teddy bears. He wanted Devon to have one of his bears, one just about as big as she was. It watched over her from a bedside table now.

There was Robby in the bed by the window. Robby was about ten years old. He had just been operated on for a large tumor in his neck. He had been diagnosed as having

Hodgkin's disease. His parents were both interested to know if we planned to follow the prescribed treatment for Devon, which was chemotherapy followed by radiotherapy. We told them that we really hadn't made the final decision, but we would probably go with the standard treatment for a Wilm's tumor.

"I don't think we are going to put Robby through all that," said his mother thoughtfully. "Have you looked into laetrile and getting treatment in Tijuana?"

I told her we had not, and deep inside I knew that we wouldn't be doing that. Call it conservative, or whatever you like. I knew we would do what was considered the best thing medically, although we were anxious to know all the alternatives included in that realm.

Since Devon seemed to be making progress toward getting out of the intensive care unit, Bill decided to return to San Diego. I would spend the days at the hospital and then drive either to Bill's sister's home or the Halbert's home for the night. I knew he needed to be back at work. His job as a guidance coordinator for the San Diego County Department of Education kept him busy consulting with many school districts. He needed to keep his contacts current in order to be an effective coordinator. But there was a strength we gave each other that I would now be without, and I longed to keep him near.

The afternoon after Bill flew back to San Diego, I sat in the hospital cafeteria toying with a coke, feeling intermittently lonely, thankful, and very weary. I became aware vaguely of the hospital paging service calling for various doctors to check in with their service. Then I suddenly realized that the last three or four names I had heard were all Devon's doctors. A little pang of fear hit my heart, and I thought perhaps I should check in on Devon. I had left her resting quietly in her bed just a while before. I made my way to the elevator.

I am convinced that God goes before us to prepare our way. It became very evident in the events that followed my stepping off the elevator on the seventh floor that afternoon. The first thing I saw was a baby crib being rushed down the hall with two nurses almost running alongside. Before I had time to ask if it was Devon, I saw that it was. One of her surgeons following at breakneck speed behind the crib paused long enough to put his arm around my shoulders and tell me that Devon was on her way to surgery. Her incision had opened from the top of her rib cage to the navel. A nurse had just discovered it a moment or so before. The Vincristine that had been administered for chemotherapy had retarded the natural healing process of the incision, which had just been held together by tape to prevent scarring.

I turned to find my way to the seventh floor waiting room. Fighting to maintain control, I made my way toward a couch. I became aware of a small lady about sixty, coming forward to where I was going to sit. In her hand she clutched a small bag. I had never seen her before, but she seemed to sense my pain and opened her arms. We hugged wordlessly. And then, I realized she was saying my name.

"Carol," she said, "it's all right. I have come to be with you. I love you." She opened up her small bag and offered me some cashews. To be polite I took one, not knowing if I could swallow anything with the large lump in my throat. From the purse she carried, she produced a wash-and-dry towelette to take care of salt on the fingertips. She explained that she too had known my brother and attended the same church as the Halberts. She understood grief, she told me, having lost both a child and a husband. As we talked together and shared the tragedies of her life and the trauma of mine, I marveled at her sensitivity to my need and her timing. I realized hers was a life used by God in service to others. The "cashew lady" was a loving message from God. He knew what we were going through. He was providing for us.

6

Coping
with Serious Illness

Sometimes it takes a while to realize that what we are going through is nothing less than a long siege. What can be done to prepare for such an experience? How can a person cope in a positive manner with an arduous ordeal? Are there approaches that can help us at times when we are unsure of the nature of the challenge facing us?

I remember sitting in the basement of one of the apartments used by married students at the University of Northern Colorado several years ago. I was discussing with three other doctoral students possible strategies for preparing for our comprehensive examinations. During "comps," as most students call them, students studying for the doctoral degree must demonstrate that they have mastery of the field of their choice. The four of us recognized that we could try to memorize our accumulated study notes from all of the classes we had ever had in psychology, but that was probably impossible. We also talked about each of us presenting to those in the group specific areas of our field as a study format. I finally decided that I needed some kind of overall grasp of the field. To do this I would study "models" that had been presented by the giants in psychology—models, for example, on intellectual development, learning, perception, psychopathology, counseling, child growth and development, moral development, healthy personality, and adult development. I would then use the appropriate models to answer the comprehensive questions on the examination and try to elaborate with details from my study notes and knowledge of research in the field.

The advantage in all of this, however, was that I was able to approach the comprehensive examinations with prior knowledge and preparation, along with some idea of the nature of past examinations. But, how do you prepare for the ordeal of cancer or any other serious illness or accident? Although we cannot begin to remove the fear, anxiety, and feelings of inadequacy as long as the stimulus for these feelings is present, there are several practical strategies which can help tremendously.

First, it is extremely helpful to become acquainted with the hospital surroundings. This sounds terribly simple, but the results are profound. In my present career as a family therapist in private practice, the very first thing I do when small children visit my office is to give them a tour of my suite. I always introduce them to my secretary, as my little clients always see her first. Sometimes I give them a job. I might say, "Let's go get the toys. You can help me carry them." It is amazing how much better they feel following our "tour."

Carol and I learned quickly that hospitals become more friendly when you know your way around them. We found out the best place to park, where the easiest entrance to the hospital was located, the idiosyncrasies of the elevator, the

best food in the cafeteria, the restroom that was more likely
to have soap, the out-of-the-way lounge that provided a
degree of privacy when needed. We familiarized ourselves
with the neighborhood immediately surrounding the hospital as well. We discovered a favorite restaurant, located a
park, and found a grocery store at which to purchase
snacks. It may not be possible to bring under control an
out-of-control illness, but it is possible to quickly bring under control your new environment.

*Second, it is possible to receive great comfort when you perceive
friends, relatives, and colleagues as a support system.* Contrary
to our thought that we might impose on those around us,
most caring people in our lives want to know what they can
do to help. They usually feel as impotent as we do and are
somewhat relieved to learn there is something they can do.
For example, we only had one car at the time of Devon's
illness. Carol's mother and father were without a car when
they flew from Denver to take care of our son, Danny, while
we were in Los Angeles with Devon. Our good friends
Harold and Dana Ayer loaned us an extra car for the duration of our stay out-of-town.

Some other friends, Monty and Athalie Okken, drove
Carol's parents and Danny to Los Angeles for a visit with us
one weekend. Other friends too numerous to mention
brought casseroles for dinner after we returned from Los
Angeles and Devon's care was transferred to the Kaiser
Hospital in San Diego. Marilyn Clark centered her attention on our son Danny. She would bring him books and
offer to take him places with her own children.

In our particular situation, it was necessary for us to
develop a new support system since Devon's surgery took
place in a city 125 miles from our home. We developed very
supportive relationships with several of the nurses at the
hospital in Hollywood, a young intern who was serving in
the pediatric ward, a wife of one of the doctors at the
hospital, and some of the other parents of children who

were patients. It is significant to note that parents of sick children often develop a close bond with one another due to the sharing of pain, grief, and anxiety.

Whether you are setting in motion an established support system or developing a new one, the fact that people care and are aware of your plight is powerfully therapeutic.

Third, it is most constructive to emphasize the "now" of an illness. Everett Shostrom in the *Manual for the Personal Orientation Inventory* indicates that the most fully functioning people (those in our midst who appear to get more out of life than most of us) strongly emphasize the present. He found that this group of people spends approximately eight out of every nine hours occupied with the present and only one out of every nine hours occupied with the past or future. He noted that those of us who are overly concerned with the past are usually filled with guilt, regret, and resentment. To the contrary, those of us preoccupied with the future are typically unrealistic and split off from what needs to be accomplished today.

If we become too engrossed with the past, we run the risk of being overwhelmed with inappropriate guilt regarding our children's illness. "Is there something we should have done which could have prevented her getting sick?" Or, "We should have spent more time with her rather than being so busy." On the other hand, if we are disproportionately concerned with the future, we can have unrealistic time goals regarding recovery.

It appears much more constructive and positive to deal with the "today segment" of the course of an illness. Being in touch with the "now" helps us to more effectively determine what can be accomplished today and assists us immeasurably in setting realistic goals for tomorrow. Setting sights on getting Devon out of the intensive care unit was much more immediately satisfying to us than trying to determine when or if she would be cured of cancer.

Fourth, it is a helpful strategy to pace yourself when faced with a serious illness. I have always been intrigued with the preparation that goes into producing a Thanksgiving dinner. We may work on the turkey and all the side dishes for more than a day. Finally, the time arrives when we all sit down to eat. We fill our plates to overflowing and probably eat more than usual. We also find out, however, that the capacity of our stomachs is pretty much the same as on any other day. So, we have to spend several days eating leftovers in order to finish off all the food that was prepared for that one meal.

A similar experience faces us when we are required to provide energy during a tragic illness. Our energy store is fairly well set regardless of the demands placed upon it. It is true that we can have a tremendous burst of energy if we are experiencing anything of an acute nature. Such a tremendous use of energy for a chronic condition, however, would only mean that over time, we are going to exhaust our energy supply. Carol and I had to learn how to pace ourselves, being careful to distribute our strength over the long haul.

We learned to prioritize our activities, emphasizing those that were most important and allowing ourselves to leave others untended. On a particularly demanding day we might take a nap to either rest from or gear up for a difficult task. We also learned to give ourselves permission to take breaks from the front lines, perhaps by going shopping or going out to dinner. Such steps were necessary in order to ensure a reserve of strength upon which we could draw to make the tough decisions, respond to adverse news regarding Devon's illness, and hold up under such a chronic physical and emotional load.

Fifth, and last, there is a great deal of comfort which comes from continued dependence upon your normal sources of strength. It might be reading an inspirational book, knitting a sweater, calling a friend, nurturing a plant you brought to the hospital from home, or praying to God for continued strength, wisdom, and courage. There is nothing quite so satisfying as testing something in which you strongly believe and finding that it is worthy of your faith.

7

Clearing Skies

*D*evon clutched my finger as she drowsily opened her eyes from the anesthesia. We were now back to step one— all the tubes back in, the very real possibilities of infection and pneumonia, and more long days in the intensive care unit.

Bill was on his way back to Los Angeles. My call had caught him at the airport via Mother and Dad. I had called home, and they had him paged at the airport. He had caught a flight back. I knew Danny would be so disappointed not to see his daddy at home that evening.

I murmured little endearments to Devon, telling her I was here, that she was loved more than words could say. I told her she would be home again soon, safe and sound with Danny and Suzy Dog. I prayed I was telling her the truth. Twice she had survived surgery. Surely God intended to spare her life.

When Bill walked through the doorway that evening, I felt new strength from his hug, and courage from his presence. It was like having fresh recruits replace the tired veteran at the front. His sister, Pat, had come to sit with us through a second recovery from surgery. We shared the trauma of the day.

That weekend my parents came to give us a break from being hospital bound. I had mixed feelings as we left for San Diego. But when I spotted the daisies freshly potted beside my front door, and opened it to go inside, I forgot for a moment the trouble that had taken me away; and I relaxed in the shelter of home. The sun was shining through a skylight and the whole room seemed to dazzle with color. Was this the same room I had regarded as old and tired looking just three weeks before? I ran my fingers over an antique table and considered how my perspective had changed.

My life had been so busy: finishing a master's degree in education with a librarianship credential at San Diego State University, decorating my home, caring for my family. Now with Devon's survival as our main concern, everything else fell away like unnecessary wrappings. *Lord, did You need my attention?* I thought. *Was I too busy with my life for You to speak clearly to me? Well, You certainly have my full attention now. What do You have in mind for us with this terrible experience?*

It was a restful weekend and over too soon. We were anxious to see Devon again. When we returned to Los Angeles Sunday afternoon, we found little Devon continuing to make progress toward her second release from the intensive care unit. We also discovered she had new roommates.

An attractive young woman was setting up "Get Well" cards and stuffed animals on the only available counter in the room. Her daughter, a thirteen-year-old, was being settled into bed by a nurse. Before the afternoon was over, the girl had suffered a seizure, one of the many that had brought her into the hospital. We learned from her parents that the doctors suspected a malignant brain tumor. While the girl's father talked to us, it was apparent that her mother was struggling to maintain her composure. How carefully we exchanged information about our daughters, each parent understanding how fragile the other's emotional state was. The looks of sympathy, the reaching out of hands to reassure each other. We told them that our prayers would be with them. They thanked us. The following morning the girl had brain surgery. When she was brought back to the intensive care unit following surgery, we realized her mother was near collapse. The outlook for their daughter was not good. Her mother was now on medication to calm her as there appeared to be little hope that their daughter would ever regain consciousness. The tumor had been too deep and widespread for surgery to eradicate.

As Bill and I left the seventh floor that day, we realized that we were certainly not alone as far as our experience was concerned. All around us other children had been stricken. Other parents were suffering the pain of sickness and possible death. Bill confided in me that he was proud of my strength and ability to cope in our situation. We both agreed that the difference was our faith in God. We sometimes felt alone, but He was there giving us strength. An evidence of God's care was our ability to not fall apart. We hadn't realized this until, through comparison, we saw someone who was struggling to cope with a hopeless situation.

We celebrated Devon's second release from the intensive care unit by buying her a lovely, long nightgown with tiny pink flowers and tiers of ruffles. I carried her around the seventh floor showing her off to nurses and parents of little patients we had come to know. She was beautiful that day; she was alive, and we were so thankful. She was scheduled for release in another week if all went well. The doctors

were hopeful that we could have a break from the hospital
for a week before she began her radiotherapy treatments as
an outpatient. I knew how we needed that week at home
before beginning the next phase of treatment. Bill returned to San Diego to sandwich in some days of work
before coming back to Los Angeles to bring us home. How
I longed for that homecoming!

Meanwhile there were some practical things to worry
about. My master's thesis was due at the printer's if I
planned to finish my degree and graduate by the end of
May. I had been trying to complete it off and on during the
hours I spent at Devon's side while she napped. The whole
thing seemed so unimportant now. But Bill encouraged
me to go ahead and try to finish.

The thesis was entitled "The Effects of Bibliotherapy on
Elementary Students' Self-Concept." It dealt with the concept of improving children's self-concept through sharing
books dealing with various problems of social development. I had been interested to discover that bibliotherapy
had been a part of ancient cultures. Even the ancient
Greeks had believed books held the possibility of healing
the soul.

I knew books could have a positive effect but even the
Bible, which had nourished my mind in the past, did not
seem relevant to the present situation. "All things work
together for good to them that love God" (Rom. 8:28, KJV)
was a verse that seemed not to include our situation. Mat-
thew 7:7 (KJV), "Ask, and it shall be given you; seek, and ye
shall find," was still unanswered in a meaningful way for
me. I felt a great impatience for God to reveal His plan and
give us assurance beyond a shadow of a doubt of Devon's
healing, or, even better, to touch her in an outright miracle.
Anything less than those two options, I really wasn't interested in. I was aware that even the doctors said we would
have two years of treatment and five years before we could

say she was cured. I was unwilling to face such a long period of uncertainty.

The day of release finally came. Release from the seventh floor prison of pain, suffering, frustration, and strange odors. Bill's mother sent money to buy candy for the nurses. As we offered it to them, I realized what emotional strain they had to go through with emergency type care required day after day. How difficult it must be to watch some children die or others leave after investing so much care.

The trip home was a victorious one. We reviewed all the experiences we had gone through, and then silently wondered about what was yet to come. Our arrival was capped off with a paper banner on the garage which read, "Welcome home Carol and Devon." Bonnie Ashman, my caring neighbor, had been at work.

As Devon and I walked up the stairs to her nursery, she put out her finger and pointed to the pictures along the way. Her smile grew in recognition of her surroundings, and she began to chatter happily. By the time she reached her own little room, she was turning this way and that noticing all the familiar toys and pictures. I smiled through my tears as I witnessed her joy at being home. I remembered my own homecoming for a weekend some weeks before. Even for a nine-month-old, there was no place like home.

The weather was mild and warm. I took Devon outside every chance we got. We went for walks, and we sunbathed on a quilt in the back yard. She loved being in her walker, which she was able to move from place to place on the patio, smelling flowers and wrinkling up her tiny nose. It was a time to store up all the sunshine and pleasure of being alive and home again.

Toward the end of the week, as the precious days at home trickled away, I gathered up a few items that we would need to establish a home away from home while Devon received her radiotherapy treatments in Los Angeles. Small apartments across the street from the hospital were provided for patients and their families who were undergoing radiotherapy. Besides the kitchen utensils and linens and clothes, I chose a few of Devon's favorite toys and a few things to feed my soul: pictures of Danny and Bill, a plant or two, and several books.

I knew how difficult it would be to make the trek back to Los Angeles. I wasn't ready to "gear up" for the next phase, which I knew would be a difficult one. There were bound to be side effects for Devon. Also, I would be absolutely on my own as Bill would need to stay in San Diego to work. We would fly home on weekends when we could.

8

Choosing
Our Response

S ooner or later the question is bound to punctuate one's conscious mind. It usually presents itself in the form of one word: Why? And then we elaborate on the theme. Why do children have to suffer? Why are some cells normal and others malignant? Why does God allow bad things to happen to good people? Why did this happen to me? Why can't the doctors find a cure?

M. Scott Peck in *The Road Less Traveled* states that one of the greatest truths for us to learn is that life is hard, it is difficult. In a statement of candor, he says,

> Most do not fully see this truth that life is difficult. Instead they moan more or less incessantly, noisily or subtly, about the enormity of their problems, their burdens, and their difficulties as if life were generally easy, as if life *should* be easy. They voice their belief, noisily or subtly, that their difficulties represent a unique kind of affliction that should not

be and that has somehow been especially visited upon them, or else upon their families, their tribe, their class, their nation, their race or even their species, and not upon others. I know about this moaning because I have done my share (p. 15).

The expression of this moaning often takes the form of the simple, one-word question: Why?

Several months ago I completed a personal study that focused on the general theme, "Why do good people suffer?" Since I was going to present my findings to an adult Sunday school class at my church, I read several books written by religious writers to gain an insight regarding my topic. After reading Harold Kushner's *When Bad Things Happen to Good People*, Edith Schaeffer's *Affliction*, and W.T. Purkiser's *When You Get to the End of Yourself*, certainly a varied group theologically, I found there are a variety of reasons given to explain suffering. In fact, the first chapter of Edith Schaeffer's book has a title that is a quantitative variation on the theme, "Why? Why? Why?" I present the most often stated answers to this question gleaned from the above authors in order to show how others grope with this question. They are presented below without comment.

1. Tragedy is probably a fairly appropriate consequence of our behavior. Sin, like bad behavior, is punished.

2. There is no rhyme or reason for suffering. It is a statistical random occurrence. There is no purpose.

3. We are a part of this world and therefore are subject to all of the possible experiences of this world.

4. Our problem is that we don't have God's view. Eventually, we will see His master plan develop.

5. Some people suffer, and some people don't. There is a kind of balance in this world that fits into God's overall scheme.

6. Tragic situations can teach us something important. God simply wants us to learn various lessons.

7. God sometimes provides us an opportunity to learn a lesson by showing us the suffering of another person.

8. Suffering is a test of your faith.

9. It really isn't right to question God. After all, God doesn't have to justify why He makes things happen.

10. When suffering occurs, there is no immediate purpose. The meaning develops and unfolds as time passes.

11. If a person is seriously ill or injured, the person may actually be the recipient of an act of mercy if the person dies.

12. Suffering allows us to get in touch with our own strength and commitment in the area of our faith.

13. God simply does not purpose everything that happens in this world. He just allows some things to happen.

In consideration of our own experience, my first attempt to grapple with this question was to become somewhat fatalistic. "Devon is a part of this world. Sickness is included in the human condition. She is not exempt from illness." Carol, on the other hand, sought to gain a spiritual insight into the purpose or plan behind Devon's cancer. Despite the contrast between our initial responses, both of us were angered by even the contemplation that God might purposely strike Devon in order to teach us something.

I am certain that most of us will always make some attempt to meaningfully answer the "Why?" of our situation. Some will be haunted and agitated until they find a plausible answer or resolve the question. Others will quietly turn to their faith for assurance that all of life has purpose and meaning.

At any rate, I'm not exactly sure how Carol and I resolved the question for ourselves so quickly, so satisfactorily as we did. The question was asked several times, but we rarely agonized over it. Perhaps it had something to do with our faith, our training, our past experiences. Perhaps it was an intuitive sense of the futility of attempting to understand completely our situation. Perhaps it was the practical aspects of our personalities and the collective wisdom of Scripture and our friends, relatives, and colleagues.

Very early during our five-month endurance of Devon's illness, we began to see wisdom in focusing on our response to our situation. It became clear that we couldn't control Devon's illness, but we could control our response to her illness. We recognized that we could be bitter, angry, negative parents or we could become positive, constructive, healthy people responding as best we could to a tragedy in our lives. Five years later, I read a paragraph by M. Scott Peck in *The Road Less Traveled* which says it very well:

> Life is a series of problems. Do we want to moan about them or solve them? Do we want to teach our childen to solve them (p. 15)?

It is beginning to be clear to me that the point at which my clients in therapy begin to successfully overcome their problems is when they begin to focus on their response and behavior rather than on a continued effort to figure out exactly how they developed their problem. A period of healthy questioning is often necessary, helpful, and therapeutic. A stagnation at this level, however, can hinder our ability to deal with our circumstances and delay our healing and recovery. Certainly, a positive response does not mean that we deny our pain, fear, frustration, anxiety. These are all feelings which at any point in time can be appropriate, but it is in spite of these feelings that we respond or behave in a positive manner.

I remember being alone with Devon one night at the hospital about eleven o'clock. Her stomach was terribly extended and she was very uncomfortable. She was having difficulty breathing. About midnight, her doctor, dressed in old street clothes, walked into her room. He had been fishing all day and had begun to think about Devon on his way home. He stopped in to see how she was doing and found me there. We chatted like two old friends who had been drawn close by mutual adversity. He became concerned about Devon's discomfort and suggested "we" might draw some of the excess fluid that was apparently collecting in her abdominal region. We talked about the pros and cons for nearly a half hour.

Finally I asked him if he really thought it would do her any good. When he indicated it might not help her, I said, "Let's don't bother with it then. It would just upset her unnecessarily." We talked some more and eventually, the doctor returned to the idea of an abdominal tap. It would have been easy for me to grow irritable, to criticize him for his indecision, or to express frustration at his inability to help her. Instead, I found myself empathizing with a doctor who so desperately wanted to help Devon that he would stop by the hospital at midnight after a long day fishing, but who had nothing in his medical repertoire with which to bring her relief. Intuitively I asked, "Would you feel better if you did the procedure?" He laughed sheepishly and admitted as much. I responded, "Let's do it then."

Many times I would hear Carol on the phone patiently and caringly answering the questions of concerned friends and worried relatives. "Yes, we are doing fine." "Today was a better day." "We were able to feed her a little bit today." "It could have happened to anybody." She rarely, if ever, hung up the phone without trying to cheer someone up or without leaving them with some sense of hope.

My mother spent a weekend with us at one point in

order to be close to us for just a few hours. Upon leaving she said, "I'm glad I came. I now know what it is really like when Carol says, 'Devon was pretty good today.'"

When adversity comes, we have many choices. We can be positive or negative. We can be helpful or critical. We can be thankful or resentful. In the midst of suffering, we can plant the seeds of recovery by deciding to respond to what life has offered us with positive, constructive behavior and at the same time become more effective in dealing with the adversity. The choice is under our control.

Part Two

THE
MIDDLE

9

Partly Cloudy

Gray was the overabiding theme for the Monday we moved into the apartments. The day was overcast in grim steel. In the dimly lit room we entered, we found the drab green of the walls and carpet blended to gray. There were the necessary furnishings, a couch, table and chairs. Standing just inside the door was a grim reminder of our purpose for being there: a child's oversized hospital bed. It was too large to be put into the bedroom and seemed incongruous with the living room. We finally settled on the dining area, which seemed a compromise.

After Bill left I found myself talking to Devon incessantly. I asked her opinion of this gray place, commented on the belongings as they were unpacked and told her about the toys I had brought along for her. She watched with large, serious eyes and listened with an air of tolerance to my ramblings. I think we both knew I was trying to fill this empty new place with human sounds.

Our first appointment for radiotherapy was set for 11:45 the next morning. I apologized to Devon for dragging her to yet another new place within twenty-four hours. With ten minutes to spare, we left our apartment and crossed the street to the hospital and the nuclear medicine facility. Later I thought it was significant that we took the elevator down to the basement for the treatment. After seeing the people who patiently waited for their treatments, it seemed appropriate that we had descended to the depths of the building.

We all shared one thing in common as we waited: an encounter with cancer. The encounters had left their mark on each one—yellow pallor, transparent skin, lack of hair or thinning hair, and eyes that looked distant. Those of us who waited with the patients shared something too—we shared an awareness of the uncertainty of life, and of the future.

Devon's name was called and a friendly looking assistant came to take her away for the treatment. Devon's face collapsed in tears and her cries echoed down the halls as she looked back at me in disbelief that I would let a stranger take her away. The other patients followed her exit with sympathetic eyes. A few minutes later she was returned, still sobbing a little.

It was like returning to life, to ascend back up to the street level. Perhaps that sounds dramatic. The emotional climate in the waiting room of nuclear medicine, however, could only be described as utterly depressing. To escape again, after the treatment, was uplifting.

I held Devon close until we were back in our apartment and then put her down for a nap. She was asleep almost immediately.

In the days that followed only the mid-day treatment broke the monotony. We seemed suspended together in time. We each only had the other. I did a great deal of reading during this time, searching for ways other people had found to cope with trauma. Catherine Marshall's book *Adventures in Prayer* was especially meaningful. She described two prayers that seemed to relate to our situation: "The Prayer of Helplessness" and "The Prayer of Relinquishment." It was easy to communicate as a helpless individual, but to relinquish this situation and Devon to His care seemed impossible. Each time I tried, my anxieties kept coming back to haunt me. I would give her to God, and then within five minutes, take up the worry where I had left off. After sharing the concept of relinquishment with Bill, I was encouraged to hear him say it sounded like I was trying to find peace through mental exercises. He felt that God was not waiting for us to pray a certain prayer, only pray and share the experience with Him. It seemed to make sense to me.

The treatments began to have their effect on Devon. First came the loss of appetite which was followed by the inability to keep anything down at all. I phoned the doctor alarmed at her vomiting, fearing that she might become dehydrated. He prescribed some medication to help her keep the food down. He also set up an appointment with the laboratory to check her blood count. The medication seemed to quiet her stomach. Devon slept in a restless manner at night now, continuously swallowing. Occasionally she would awaken with a terrible cry, and I would race in from my bed. My heart pounding, I would pick her up to see what was wrong. After holding her awhile, letting her wake up and quiet her crying, she would lie back down. I wondered what terrible dream or pain or memory she had just endured.

There was a daily call from Bill and my mother. Occasionally there would be a welcomed visit from Bill's sister or my cousin who lived in Los Angeles. I knew what an effort it was for both of them since both were working women. Free time for them was at a minimum. My dad had now returned home to Denver to take care of a house and yard that had been left vacant for six weeks. How selfless it had been for my parents to come and help us for weeks on end. Friends sent little notes of encouragement through the mail. These all were the threads that held me to the other world, the one peopled with healthy folks, going about their lives in an ordinary way.

One afternoon as Devon and I were crossing the street midblock from the hospital to the apartment, I noticed a motorcycle policeman coming our way, but still some distance up the street. I hesitated on the curb a moment, then proceeded to cross the street. As I hurried on across, I was surprised to hear a siren begin to blow, and even more surprised when the motorcycle drove into the apartment complex driveway and blocked my path. My face must have registered shock as I realized that the siren had been for me, and I waited to hear what he had to say.

"Lady!" the policeman said with hostility accenting the first syllable. "You saw me coming and you went right ahead and broke the law anyway. You knew better than to jaywalk!"

I explained to him that I had rather absentmindedly looked for a shortcut across the narrow street, but had not purposely broken the law. When I had hesitated on the curb, I think I was judging whether or not to let him pass before crossing. I went on to explain that my daughter had cancer and that we were presently involved in radiotherapy which often took us across the street. Because she was ill, I wanted to get her home as quickly as possible. I finished my explanation and then asked if I could proceed to the apartment.

"No! I'm not finished with you yet," was his reply. "If you were to get hit with a car, it would compound your present problems, wouldn't it?" he said sarcastically.

By then I was becoming very angry. I made no attempt to hide my irritation, when I said, "If you are going to give me a ticket, do it. And for heaven's sake, let me get this sick child inside out of the wind."

"With a person like you, it wouldn't do any good at all!" he retorted angrily. With a roar of his engine, he was gone to leave me fuming.

Angry tears formed in my eyes as I walked quickly into the apartments. How totally lacking in empathy the man had been. As I sat Devon down on the floor to play, I tried to decide what to do. Should I call the police department and complain? I had noted his badge number while we talked. I finally decided to take the same course of action he had. Why report it? With a person like that, it would probably do no good! I knew that in my mind he would forever remain the "policeman without a heart."

The incident was all but forgotten by the following weekend when graduation day dawned clear and beautiful. Devon and I were home for the weekend. I would go through the ceremonies at San Diego State University and officially receive my master's degree. The thesis had made it to the copiers and the printers in time. Now a bound volume stood on a shelf somewhere in the large San Diego State library and one volume was on our own bookshelf. It was impressive in its black binding, but amazingly thin for all the work involved.

Bill had arranged for my dad to fly to San Diego for the day, and Bill's mother had flown in from San Francisco. Bill confided that he wanted it to be a special day for me, to make up in part for all I had been through. How much I loved him in that moment for all his care and sensitivity. Friday when Devon arrived home, he had insisted we take a trip to the jewelers to select a new watch in honor of the graduation on Sunday.

Although Devon would stay at home with a friend during the proceedings, I felt like it was a day that should involve her, too. All the time I had been pregnant, I had attended classes. The daily trips to the library for a difficult reference class had been when I was seven months along in my pregnancy. She would probably be at home in a library some day, I thought. The fall after her birth, I continued classes part time. Each morning I would take Devon to a neighbor who cared for her while I was in class. After class I would come to pick her up and with smiles all around, we would spend the rest of the day together. Books would be put away for a while, and we would spend some time relaxing. Then the typewriter would put her to sleep for her afternoon nap.

As I bathed her now, I was cautious as I drew the washcloth over the eight-inch scar that had given us such problems earlier. She will have to wear one-piece bathing suits when she grows up, I reasoned. We selected a pale yellow dress that Grandma Cherry had brought with her from San Francisco. Now she would look beautiful for the picture-taking session to follow.

Checking my new watch, I decided it was time to wake Danny up. I found he was already up and dressed. He would attend the graduation with us. As we went outside for pictures, the morning sun turned his blond hair to gold. Cameras snapped the graduate and her handsome son together. I remembered Danny's statement as a little boy when someone had complimented him, saying how handsome he was. He had corrected them with "handsome as a prince." His self-concept had faltered a bit during the last three months, however. For the first time in his school years, he had begun having problems. Because of his apparent need to have teacher help on all his work, he had been moved back to a lower reading group. The teacher felt he might be more comfortable and less dependent on her for help. He had always been a strong reader. He had learned to read when he was four, quite effortlessly. When Bill talked with the teacher, he discovered it was more a need on Danny's part for reassurance rather than not knowing the answers. He needed a special touch and warmth and had figured out a way to find it: a mother's touch at school while his own mother was away from home. He was put back in the appropriate reading group. Subsequently he was tested for a gifted class and qualified easily. Summer was coming soon, and we would be a family again. I couldn't wait.

Under a cloudless sky that Sunday in May, the graduates filed into the San Diego State football field. I was feeling a little proud of the blue hood I wore which signified the field of education. Because of the large number of graduates, individual names were not read. Each department was presented and asked to stand. At long last after sitting under a very hot sun, the candidates for the master's degree in education were asked to stand. We all stood and gave a somewhat wilted cheer. Then it was over. It had been a nice way to say "finished" to a difficult two years.

The following Monday morning as I strapped Devon into her car seat, after our flight from San Diego to Los Angeles, I reflected on the great weekend at home. It had been wonderful to have something positive to capture our attention for a change. *Now back to reality,* I thought as I put the key into the ignition. I turned it, but absolutely nothing happened. I had left the car in front of the Halbert's home and they had driven me to the airport on Friday. Now, as I looked at my watch, I realized that they were both at work. I turned the key again, and the engine barely turned over. It sounded like the battery was dead. My heart sank and a prayer began to form.

"Please, Lord, help the car to start. I am all alone. No one is home to help me, and Devon's radiotherapy appointment is pretty soon." I turned the key again and again with the same results each time. Nothing. Wasn't it enough that this child beside me had gone through so much, that we

were struggling all alone in a strange city, and that in an
hour we would have to descend to the depths for a treatment? Why did the car have to act up? Why couldn't the
Lord give us a little assistance here?

Putting what was left of my good sense to work and
wiping the tears that kept filling my eyes, I looked around
the neighborhood, trying to select a house that didn't appear too unfriendly. I would have to ask to use someone's
phone and call the Halberts at work or Triple A.

An hour later the Triple A truck had come and gone,
the appointment had been rescheduled and we were on
our way to our apartment. Perhaps it had been important
that day for an old man to feel useful while I used his
phone and told him all our troubles. Maybe the Lord
needed to let me know of my own ability to work out life's
irritations. Whatever the reason, if in fact there needed to
be a reason, I knew even as a Christian, I wasn't exempt
from the problems and frustrations of life.

The next morning as I was washing Devon's hair, I realized that those beautiful curls were coming out in my hand.
Call it vanity if you like, but those dark curls meant a lot to
me. I could hardly finish bathing her. I kept thinking of all
the times in the store when people had stopped to comment on her beautiful hair. It was a symptom of her treatment we had expected, but one which we had hoped
wouldn't appear. It affected me more than the vomiting or
lack of appetite, both of which had been somewhat con-
trolled by medication. Now she was physically changed.
That afternoon when we sat with the others in the nuclear
medicine waiting room, she looked like she belonged
there. We hadn't lost the battle, but losing some of her
physical beauty seemed like a victory for cancer. After her
nap later that day, we began a bonnet search together. I
found two that were cute, but somehow they didn't help
her look like Devon.

Coming back to the apartment one day the same week, we encountered our next-door neighbor, a lady from San Diego who had recently had a uterine operation for cancer. Now she was taking a series of radiotherapy treatments. I asked her how she was feeling and if she had experienced the usual symptoms of nausea and diarrhea. Her answer sounded determined but unrealistic.

"I haven't experienced any of those symptoms and I don't intend to experience them. I believe in mind over matter."

Several times after that visit our paths crossed. When asked how she was doing, each time she answered a confident "Fine." Her step was brisk, her manner sure, and she looked well and strong.

With butterflies in my stomach and Devon in my arms, I handed the Manila envelope to the oncologist following four weeks of radiotherapy treatment. As he opened it and took out the x-rays of Devon's chest and abdomen, I scarcely breathed. I watched his face for clues. A frown momentarily passed his forehead. My stomach gave a lurch. It was the first set of x-rays taken since the surgery. There would be many more to follow after each series of chemotherapy treatments during the next two years.

"All clear!" the doctor said. "The x-rays show Devon to be clear of disease." With that he looked up to see my response. My thanks poured forth and I shook his hand.

The news he had just given us meant that Devon and I were free to return to San Diego. We would have four weeks at home before the next series of chemotherapy treatments began. All further treatments would take place in San Diego. Devon could either be hospitalized for each series or come in as an outpatient.

My heart was full of thanksgiving. The Lord had given us a wonderful answer to prayer. I felt reborn with hope.

The worst was surely over now. I dared not think of the uncertain months ahead, when there would be more treatments and more x-rays. For the moment it was enough to know that Devon was one step closer to health.

10

Nurturing
Ourselves and Others

*I*t is difficult to know just how to respond to people who are deeply engulfed in a fight for life. The majority of us arrive at a single question when we are considering our own response to someone with a serious illness. The question is, "What should I say?" It is an interesting observation that at that moment we are focusing on ourselves rather than the one who needs comforting. Our intent for the most part is honorable, but we struggle with our inadequate knowledge about what feels good to someone racked with emotional pain.

It may be helpful to know that those of us who have experienced serious illnesses or accidents usually don't anticipate or expect comfort from those strangers who momentarily enter our lives during the course of our experience. For example, words of comfort from a grocery clerk, a mother of a colleague whom you've never met, the parents of another patient, the owner of a house where you made an emergency phone call, or an acquaintance you have really never known very well, can often be surprising.

Although we do not expect comfort from these people, neither do we expect harsh insensitivity as in the case of the traffic control officer Carol encountered in Hollywood. However, that officer is a rarity. Few people handle their discomfort by being harsh, irritable, angry, insensitive, and uncaring.

During Devon's illness, it was typical to wish for some "good news." By this I mean news of a positive nature from others in our lives. Often Carol or I would ask if we had gotten any mail, hoping for some "good news." However, if someone reported even a minute negative experience, we might say, "More bad news!" On the other hand, if we received a card, a letter, or a word of comfort from someone with whom we had no close ties, it was always experienced as unexpected "good news."

Most of us don't agonize over our response to people we don't know very well. We sense that anything we do as a gentle gesture for someone in such a situation is really more than would be expected. Where we tend to experience discomfort is with friends we do know well and with whom we have a significant relationship. We know we need to respond and we want to respond, but we don't know how.

It was our experience throughout Devon's illness that most, if not all, of our friends and relatives sincerely, desperately wanted to provide us with comfort. In fact, several of our friends who met in a study group each week asked Carol and me to share our thoughts about our experience. One of the questions raised was, "How can we respond in a positive way to people going through your experience?" In an effort to lend insight to this question and to assist us all in responding to friends and acquaintances in similar situations in the future, perhaps it might be useful to share first what was comforting, helpful, and healing to us. Then, second, to provide some recommendations or suggestions for responding to others in a positive way.

Our friends, relatives, and colleagues responded to us in a variety of ways. All of them appeared to be genuine and caring. Some responses, however, were less comforting than others. There were those who would spend time with us or even make a nice gesture of some kind, but never broach the subject of Devon's illness. These caring folk would often come to our home, maybe spend an hour, and talk about the weather, the neighborhood, the upcoming holiday plans, school—everything except what was the only thing on our minds and what was the motivation for their visit. We always appreciated these friends as they were trying their best to make meaningful contact with us. We have since learned that these good people often were operating under the assumption that we wouldn't want to talk about Devon and it would help to "take our minds off of the situation." To the contrary, the single most therapeutic thing for us to do at that time was to talk about Devon. Usually, we would have to start talking about her. If we didn't, they would finally end the conversation and leave our home as though they had been through another neighborly chat. Nevertheless, we appreciated these people because we knew why they were there in our home.

Some of our friends would approach us and openly confess their feelings of inadequacy. "Oh, I just don't know what to say. I'm so sorry. I know I can't do anything, but if I can, let me know." We felt positive about these people simply because it does help to know that others whom you care about are aware of your plight. We always thanked them for their concern and their expressions of thoughtfulness. Such a response, however, usually led to our having to comfort them regarding their feelings of inadequacy. We might say, for example, "Don't worry about it. There isn't much to say. It's difficult for all of us." On several occasions, some of our friends would thank *us* for making *them* feel better.

Then there were those who felt the need to leave us with some thought, poem, verse of Scripture, or idea that would provide us an explanation or reason why we were going through a trying time. I remember the day when an acquaintance we had known years before came to town and heard about Devon. She made a special effort to call, and it would have been much easier for her to neglect such a gesture as we had never been close friends and hadn't even had contact for some fifteen years. I am thankful she called. Unfortunately she took the time to quickly express her understanding as to the reason why Devon was ill. In a sincere effort to be helpful, she said to Carol, "God certainly must be refining you and Bill for something wonderful." Well, that might be a true statement. But, when I heard about it, I was discomforted by the thought that my little girl would suffer in order for Carol and me to get in shape for some special task in the future.

There are no "quick-fix" answers for those who are suffering. To even attempt to give a simple explanation for the purpose of such a complex event is to generally be doomed to failure, and in my case, cause additional pain. Providing comfort is one thing; providing philosophy is something else.

I will forever be grateful to the people who knew there wasn't much they could do, who felt no pressure to explain it all to us, who if they felt inadequate didn't focus on it, but decided instead to simply, quietly, share the burden with us.

Bob and Jo Bell invited us to have a brunch with them one Sunday morning as their guests. They made sure Danny was welcome, and we shared a sensitive time together talking about Devon, our emotional ups and downs, our fears, and our hope. I basked in what felt like an envelope of care as they unhurriedly gave us the impression that they were ready to spend the entire day with us if it would help.

Then there was Bill Clarke, a colleague of mine who was working with me in a large high school district to create an improved guidance program. One morning in San Diego, Devon was particularly uncomfortable, and I had stopped by the hospital to be with her. I was supposed to chair the meeting but called Bill to tell him to start the meeting without me. I would be there as soon as possible. About an hour later, I finally entered the room where the meeting was being conducted. I was dreading the effort it would take to walk in the room as though everything were normal, pick up the leadership reins, and begin creative work. Instead, as soon as I sat down, Bill turned to me and said, "Bill, all of these people know what's going on, they know where you have just been, and they all care. If it would help, why don't you share how things went this morning." I found myself sharing the morning with those wonderful people who were willing to set aside their priorities in order to share my pain. I felt the tension leaving my body, and then, miraculously, I was ready to work. Bill knew Devon was the only thing on my mind, gave me a chance to deal with it, and provided me with a supportive group in which to share. Energy returned to me, and I was then able to meet the requirements of the day.

I will never forget Ron Hockwalt. Intuitively, Ron seemed to know that the most helpful thing he could "do" for me was to "be" with me. When Devon was transferred to the Kaiser Hospital in San Diego for her care, Ron would stop by the pediatric ward about 5:30 P.M. on his way home from work. He would spend ten or fifteen minutes chatting with us about the day.

One day, I was late stopping by the hospital and Carol had already gone home to fix dinner. I walked into the ward, walked down the hall, and then I saw Ron. He was carrying Devon in his arms, walking her all around the ward. When he saw me he said, "I came in and nobody was here. Devon seemed to want to be held so I picked her up. I hope it's okay."

With emotion welling up in my heart, I told him it was fine! I left the hospital that evening feeling loved, cared for, and comforted. Ron left me with the true standard of friendship: someone who enters another's world and shares not only the joy, but the sorrow. A phrase from a note Ron sent us was full of meaning: "As your friends, we share your pain."

Are there any guidelines that can help us comfort our friends in need? There are several. *Perhaps the most helpful suggestion is to focus on the person being comforted.* To focus on ourselves is to get in touch with our feelings of inadequacy. Focusing on the person in pain, however, can assist greatly in helping us determine what to say and what we might be able to do to bring comfort. Focusing on the person as a priority means we will be looking at them and listening carefully to them. If they look really fatigued, for example, we may be able to offer some kind of help related to the need for rest. One of our friends offered to spend time with Danny and Devon in order to allow us time to get away from the pressures of constant care and concern. Listening to someone in need helps us to know what to say. We simply respond to what they are saying rather than try to initiate some creative, unique, imaginative phrase that wraps the problems up in a package with a bow.

Most of us have a hard time doing this and this puts us in touch with our inadequacies. I remember reading two cards sent to us during Devon's illness. One friend said, "I've been waiting for some words to come, but none have." Another admitted, "I'm not very good with words." What these people didn't realize is that no one needs to be profound. The fact that they knew of our situation and communicated their care was all that we needed.

The dialogue for providing comfort can be relatively simple. It might go something like this:

"Hi, how are things going?"

"Oh, Judy, we've been trying our best to hold things together."

"That must be really hard. I'm just really sorry you're having to go through this."

In just three short sentences by Judy, she has communicated her interest, her care, and the fact that she has heard what it is like to be in the other person's situation. In our experience, such an interaction with caring friends was tremendously comforting.

Focusing on the person you want to comfort can give you keys to helpful behavior. For instance, if you have dropped by to visit the person and he appears very tired, it would be appropriate to stay but a few minutes. The length of stay is not the crucial point. The fact that you cared enough to stop by lets the person know what you wanted to communicate: "I care." On the other hand, if it appears the person feels like talking, you might want to extend your stay longer than you had previously planned.

Another suggestion is to recognize that the emotions being experienced by people in pain are normal and appropriate. Many of us seem to think others are not doing very well if they are sad, cry occasionally when they are talking, or appear to have little energy. So, we try to be cheerleaders. There is nothing wrong with expressions of hope. Cheerleading, however, implies the often simplistic idea that relief is but a positive thought away. The problem with that idea is that relief is not easily achieved in the midst of serious illness or accident. Reality may suggest that the outcome can be very much in doubt. One of our friends, for example, told us that he was sure everything would be fine if we would just have faith in our doctor. "He knows what he is doing," he said.

Well, our doctors would have been the first to admit that Devon's life was in jeopardy and the outcome was in doubt. We recognized the naiveté of our friend's remark, but thanked him anyway. The danger, however, is that we sometimes make people feel as though their feelings are inappropriate, wrong, or a sign of weakness. The more comforting approach is to allow their feelings, let them express them, and respond accordingly. "I'm so sorry this is happening to you." Or, "I feel so sad about all of this. Would you like to talk about it?"

Another guideline is to recognize that talking about difficulties can be tremendously therapeutic for those going through a painful experience. Many people would approach Carol and me by saying, "I know you don't want to talk about it, but I want you to know I'm thinking about you." Well, that wasn't always true. Sometimes the most helpful thing for me was to share what I was thinking and experiencing. Recently a friend of mine told me she had a neighbor who had lost her three-month-old baby. My friend had been calling her on the phone just to talk about it. She asked me if that were okay. I told her that it might very well be just what her neighbor needed. But I said to her, "Why don't you ask your neighbor to be sure?" Some of the most helpful people I experienced were those who asked me if I would like to talk about Devon and then allowed me to make the decision.

"Hi, how's it going?"

"Oh, I sure wish all of this were over."

"Would it help to talk about it?"

"I'm really talked out right now."

"That's fine. Let me know if you would like to talk."

Sometimes we are trying to be comforting but what we are really doing is forcing the person to give us a full medical report everytime we see them. This can be very tiring, especially if everyone asks for a complete update. Usually,

the person has a few very close friends who by the nature of
their relationship, know all the details. During Devon's illness, Donna Dennis was one of those persons in our life.
We later found out that several of our friends would call
her for the medical details and limit their discourse with us
to expressions of comfort and care. Donna played an
important role for both of us as well as for friends who
wanted to know about us but not burden us with questions.
Of course, Carol's parents often played the role of letting
people know what was going on since they were living in
our home taking care of Danny while we were with Devon
in Los Angeles.

*Perhaps the most important suggestion is simply to be sure you
let someone know you care.* The "quality" of the expression
isn't nearly as important as the fact that you have made
contact. One person in my life waited for five months before making any contact with me. When he finally did, his
reason was that he didn't know what to say. The sad thing
about that is that I knew better than anyone that there
really wasn't much to say. But, then, the comfort is making
some kind of contact. If it's a card, note, or letter, include
just a sentence or two regarding your thoughts. As terrible
as it may sound, I found myself quickly discarding cards
from people who depended on a professional writer's verse
to comfort me. In fact, I rarely even read the verse. What I
was desperately hungry for was the sentence or two that let
me know someone had Carol and me in mind. We still have
those cards and review them about once each year.

A word about the least helpful manner in which comfort
is attempted might be important. Advice is generally a
waste of time and can be damaging at times. As a therapist,
I have learned time and time again that I am the least
therapeutic and helpful when I am giving advice. As much
as we think we can, we can never fully comprehend or
understand exactly what it's like to be another person.

Therapists spend a career trying to become experts at being empathetic, trying to enter and appreciate another's life space.

Just last week a client of mine who is Japanese was trying to tell me what his life has been like: parents who were placed in internment camps during World War II, being the butt of ethnic jokes, being taught to deny his heritage by blending, being made to feel that he was not quite at the same level as his colleagues, not for what he can or cannot do, but for who he is. A few days before our visit someone at his place of work was organizing a party to watch the final episode of *M.A.S.H.*, the television program. My client was invited to the party this way: "We want you to come as the enemy." Finally, my client looked at my Anglo face and said, "Bill, you will never really know what I have gone through."

If I had been a novice therapist, I probably would have tried to refute his statement. Instead, I agreed with him. I said, "Don, you're right. I'll never know what it's like to be an ethnic minority in a culture in which the majority is Anglo. But, I do know something of what it is like to feel different." As a small boy, I had to grow up in a broken home before it was commonplace to do so. I remember having to complete one of those cards which begin, "In case of emergency, please contact. . . ." The first line asked for the name and address of my father. I didn't know what to do. Finally, I went to the teacher and asked, "I don't have a father. Is that okay?" She told me it was fine and to just complete the line where it asked for my mother's name and address. I still felt different, but comforted to know not having a father was "okay."

What I have learned and what Don reminded me about is that we can't truly, completely know what another person is going through unless we are that person. But we can in some measure identify with the feelings that person is experiencing. Therefore, I can comfort, but I can't advise. I can no more tell Don what he should do with his ethnic heritage than I can tell someone how they should respond to a life-threatening ordeal. Actually, it can be somewhat comforting to know that we are not required to come up with advice—that we need only to comfort and to care.

Finally, just a word or two about a couple of aspects relating to the response Carol and I experienced with each other. We were fortunate to be able to alternately draw strength from each other. There were times when Carol would feel particularly vulnerable, and she would draw strength from me. There were just as many times when the opposite was true. I needed her to supply the energy for us to go on. A good example was on the day we learned Devon had cancer. I had been working with the doctors all day as they were trying to come up with a definitive diagnosis. Carol spent a lot of that day crying. She finally said to me, "Bill, I'm so sorry. I just can't stop crying. You just seem to be so strong." I told her not to worry about it and that she certainly didn't have to feel guilty for crying. That evening, however, she notified our relatives and close friends by phone that Devon had cancer. I was unable to make even one phone call because I couldn't stop crying.

Family therapists have learned through research and clinical practice that some of the healthiest marital relationships are those in which husbands and wives "respond" to each other. When one or the other feels vulnerable, for example, the other fills in where needed. Such a relationship allows each spouse to sometimes supply the strength and sometimes to borrow from the strength of the other. A less healthy relationship would be one in which one person always has to play the strong role and the other always has to play the weak role. The experience of our response to each other meant that we were never both "down" at the same time. What a relief it is to work as "one" in the midst of an ordeal. Parents of ill children can really benefit from each other by allowing an honest response to an ordeal. Requiring each to play a set role in an exclusive manner can have devastating consequences.

Carol and I responded to Devon's illness by holding on to the idea that our individual lives continued to be important. It wasn't necessary or shameful for us to meet our needs or discontinue our dreams and projects in light of Devon's illness. It would have been easy for Carol to delay or even give up on her effort to finish her master's degree at San Diego State University. It made sense to us, however, to believe that we would be better able to meet Devon's needs if some of our needs were met.

Carol once heard a psychologist talking to a group of teachers. During his presentation, he made an insightful comment. "You will never be able to fill your children's love buckets unless your own love bucket is full." That became our philosophy in response to life during Devon's crisis. Carol needed a positive experience to be able to better respond during a negative period in our lives. If we needed a break from child care, we asked someone to care for Danny and Devon. If we needed a distraction from our situation, we would go out to dinner. If we needed to feel particularly close, we would make love.

A significant lesson to learn in life is the fact that we often feel closest to others when we are sharing the pain of the human condition. We respect and compliment those who have it together, and we walk away feeling inferior. But, we love and comfort those who are hurting, and we can walk away feeling a part of another's healing process.

11

The Gathering Storm

I watched Devon smile at her big brother as he entertained her in his play yard. Her brightest smiles seemed to be reserved for Danny and his antics. Just now she sat in her walker watching Danny dig elaborate tunnels and caves in the sand and then crash them down with his army men in mock battle. The accompanying battle sounds kept her attention riveted on him.

We had been home for a month now. My brother and his family had come from Oklahoma for a visit and to meet for the first time the object of their prayers during the last few months—little Devon. I felt cheated that the Devon they were meeting was pale and nearly bald. But the dark eyes and demure smile charmed them just the same. One thought that had continually nagged at me during their visit was whether or not Devon's appetite was declining. I tried to convince myself that perhaps she was distracted by the house full of company. But after Roger and his family left for Los Angeles, it became apparent that she was not eating well. Not only that, but now she was running a low-grade fever in the afternoon. Icy fingers of fear crept into my heart. I called the pediatrician for an appointment. The appointment was set for July fifth.

While Devon napped upstairs, Bill and I and other parents in our neighborhood wove red, white, and blue crepe paper through wheels of tricycles, bicycles, and wagons. It was the annual Fourth of July Parade, and on the morning of the all-important holiday, the garage was a patriotic sea of children and their vehicles in the appropriate colors. Later in the afternoon following the children's parade, a balloon toss, three-legged race, and other festivities would sharpen the appetites of all involved for the block barbeque and picnic.

As soon as the dark shadows of evening filled the cul-de-sac, the sparklers would be handed out and a few rockets fired off by adults to cap off the celebration.

When the last bike was wheeled proudly out of the garage and its owner tooted a party horn, I slipped upstairs to dress Devon for the occasion. Her face felt warm as I slipped a red, white, and blue sun suit over her head. I tried to keep my growing alarm in check. This was a special afternoon, and we would enjoy it.

Several neighbors greeted Devon as we walked down the street to set up tables for the picnic. A large sheet cake adorned one of the tables. As I took a closer look I realized it was a "Happy Birthday" cake with Devon's name on it and also Grandpap's. Grandpap, an elderly man in the neighborhood, would be ninety during July, and Devon would be one year old in just eighteen more days. *God grant that Devon will have many more July Fourths to celebrate and birthday cakes to admire,* I thought. I kissed her warm face.

The next afternoon, following a morning of bloodwork

and x-rays, the telephone rang in our upstairs bedroom. It was Devon's doctor.

"Mrs. Rowley, I have just completed going over Devon's tests, and I have some very disappointing news. The x-rays show that there is a return of the disease in the lungs. The cancer has metastasized throughout both lungs. I would suggest that you bring her in tomorrow and we will start a chemotherapy series of massive dosage."

When the phone had rung, I had been playing with Devon on our bed. I realized that I couldn't face her or bear to look at her. I called Bill and asked that he take her into her room. My stomach felt uneasy. A sense of great anger overtook me. As I took the receiver back again to finish the conversation, I heard my harsh voice saying, "Why bring her in for treatment? What good would it do? We have done exactly what we were supposed to do, and look where it has gotten us! Why subject this poor child to any more pain or treatment? She is going to die anyway!"

Bill took the phone away from me. After several more minutes of conversation, I heard him agree to one more series of chemotherapy treatments.

A hot, humid night had fallen. Upstairs the box fan hummed endlessly trying to supply comfort and coolness to the restless sleepers. I knelt beside a chair in the darkened living room and felt the tears falling even before my knees touched the floor. I poured out my prayers to God. I had believed God loved Devon even more than I did. If so, was He crushed with the thought of her further suffering? How would I be able to watch her suffer, grow weaker, and die? Was it possible He could still touch her and free her of the cancer? What words could I use to express to Him the Gethsemane I was going through?

When I got up from the chair some time later, I felt exhausted, unable to cry or pray further. I had told God everything that was in my heart. There was nothing left inside that hadn't been stated. Now the whole thing was in

His corner. I slept deeply through the night, in spite of the heat, but I awakened with a sense of foreboding. For a moment I lay still. Then I remembered: my daughter was dying.

Reluctantly I agreed to try one more chemotherapy series as a last-ditch effort for Devon. The doctor had told us that there might still be a chance it could be effective, if the cancer had not spread further than the lungs. While she was in for the chemotherapy, there would also be some tests to determine if her abdomen was clear of disease. I hid a little hope deep in my heart. Even now when faced with the impossible odds for Devon's recovery, I still found myself praying for a miracle.

After being admitted to the hospital, we were shown to the same room overlooking the roof garden that we had occupied in April. How much we had gone through since that first discovery! What was our future in this room? I couldn't bring myself to contemplate it.

At the sound of voices in the hall, I looked around to see who was speaking louder than the usual hospital hush. Bill was having a very intense discussion with a radiologist from the Los Angeles hospital who had come to San Diego to check on patients who had been radiated at the Los Angeles facility. I was immediately on my guard, remembering his colleague's abrupt manner when we questioned him regarding radiotherapy for Devon last spring.

Later Bill gave me the capsulized version of the conversation. The radiologist assumed we would be bringing Devon to Los Angeles again for further radiation since the cancer had recurred. Bill told him that we would be staying in San Diego. At such a difficult time, we would need our support system of family and friends intact here in San Diego.

The radiotherapist had then accused Bill of being selfish and not giving Devon every chance to survive. Bill told him that if radiation was indicated that we would have a private clinic in San Diego do it since it wasn't one of the services the local Kaiser Hospital offered. In our view there was good enough reason for the hospital health plan to fund and allow Devon to receive radiotherapy from a private clinic. Bill then told him he didn't appreciate his accusation regarding our attitude. No one cared more about Devon's healing than we did, and no one but us knew what we had already gone through for her. Bill was so enraged that he refused to allow him to examine Devon or to treat her in the future.

My thoughts drifted back to my own protectiveness toward Devon and other experiences we had gone through with medical personnel. Some had been caring and sensitive, others cold and businesslike. Perhaps a confrontation was necessary; these professionals really do need to know some of the pain that families go through at times like this.

The following afternoon I shut my car door and hurried up the walk to the hospital. If I hurried maybe I could entice Devon to take a little food. Her appetite was almost nonexistent.

"Wait a minute, Carol. I'll walk up with you," called a good friend. "Here, I brought something for our little lamb Devon." She handed me a fleecy white stuffed animal. I hugged her tight and felt the ever-present lump in my throat move closer to the surface. In answer to her questions of how Devon was today, I explained that we were to get the results of tests she had undergone to determine the range of the new cancer. If it were present in the abdomen, then further chemotherapy or radiation would be considered fruitless. She would be considered terminal.

As we walked into Devon's second-floor room, her doctor was waiting for me. He explained that the scan showed the cancer was now present in the liver as well as the lungs.

Fighting to hold tears in check, I fled from the room. My friend hurried after me, tears streaming down her face as well.

"Carol, I'm so sorry, so sorry," she said. "Would you let me drive you home? Are you okay?"

"I'll be all right, but I need to be alone now. Thank you anyway. Oh, and thanks for the little lamb for Devon."

In my heart I wondered how long those little fingers would pet that fleecy lamb.

The three ministers and three church leaders filed around the hospital crib. Devon slept through their quiet entrance. The senior pastor anointed her with a little olive oil. Each man bowed his head and our good friend Monty began to pray. It was a strong prayer of faith. Numbly, I listened. There had been so many prayers offered already. There had been so many places where God's healing and intervention could have taken place, but no such miracle had taken place. Perhaps my father's summary of the situation months ago had been accurate: a cold and cancer were of the same magnitude to God. If He chose not to heal her then it was a part of a higher plan, certainly not comprehensible to us.

The prayer was now finished. Bill and I thanked them for coming. Devon had awakened midway through the prayer; and, startled to see so many strange faces, she had begun to cry. I reached out to reassure her and held her little hand. I studied it now, with its bruises and needle marks. I knew that unless God intervened, I could not subject her to more treatment. We would take her home to die, surrounded by a loving family.

Interacting
with Significant Others

P arents of a terminally ill child are presented with difficult and somewhat ironic roles to play as they interact with some rather significant others in their lives. Those significant people include any remaining children, doctors assigned to the case, and ministers of the family.

Perhaps living life to the full means that we confront all that life provides, take full advantage of opportunities presented, and rest in the fact that we have done our best with what has been offered in spite of any mistakes we have made. In his book *Identity: Youth and Crisis*, Erik Erikson, one of the leading professionals in the field of psychoanalysis and human development, suggested that such people develop a sense of integrity during their later years of life. These experienced, mellow, mature individuals can look back on life with a sense that "all is well." The alternative, of course, is to run from life, to meet it passively, to refrain from risking yourself in new experiences. When this happens, stagnation occurs. Erikson believed that these people develop a sense of despair in their later years, accompanied with feelings of guilt, resentment, and regret.

How do you sensitively talk with other children in your family about the fact that their brother or sister is dying? How do you deal with doctors who have pledged to keep their patients alive but who are losing the battle? What do you say to a minister who is suggesting the need for a continuing faith, but who feels as helpless as you do? Difficult experiences, all, and they are thrust on the families of children who are dying.

There is a special uniqueness about parents having to face the death of a child. Psychologically, it flies against the normal pattern of the life cycle. Children expect their parents to die first; and, under normal circumstances, they do. In fact, some psychologists believe that most of us refrain from considering our own death until our parents die. They seem to provide us with a psychological buffer of safety. The unconscious thought runs something like, *I won't die until after my parents are gone.* To be faced with the very real possibility that our child will die means that we have to somehow communicate with other children in our family about a subject that we are struggling with ourselves. Simply put, it seems all wrong. But talk to them we must.

INTERACTING WITH OTHER CHILDREN

Naturally, it is most effective if we have the chance to talk to our children about death before any such occasion arises. Most of us understand and accept the concept of death even though reflecting on our own personal death might be another matter. We recognize that all living things die. None of us is personally acquainted with a neighbor who has lived forever. We are born, we develop, (some of us get married and have children), we grow old, and we die. This process happens continually all around us. We can count on it. Even our folklore includes the saying, "You can be sure of death and taxes."

Therefore, we can talk with our children about the idea that death is a very natural part of living. We can show them the cycle of life by looking at plants, talking about pets whose lives have come to an end, and by discussing death when someone dies. However, we must recognize that children do not understand the full meaning of death until they are around seven or eight years old. When we talk to children about death we also need to reassure them that life goes on. And if we have a faith, we can include our beliefs about the eternal nature of life. Gradually, over a period of time, as circumstances provide opportunity, the idea of death can be dealt with in a positive manner, stressing the naturalness of it. Such preparation prior to a death that hits close to home can really help children to resolve the death of someone they know and love in a constructive way.

In our case, we started with an illness about which the final outcome was unknown. We began with the idea that the doctors might find Devon's tumor benign during surgery. But her illness progressively worsened until hope was gone. In looking back on our efforts to share Devon's illness with our son, Danny, our behavior centered around several key concepts. These ideas may be helpful as guidelines for others who have a similar experience in the future.

Guidelines

1. Everything we said to Danny was centered around the truth as we knew it. We essentially told him no more but no less than we knew. For example, when we knew Devon had cancer but were still hopeful of healing, we told Danny that she was very ill, but that we were doing everything possible to make her well again. We did not tell him she would get well, but we didn't tell him she would die either. At that point in time, we truthfully didn't know which outcome would occur. Instead, we told him what we did know and what we were trying to do about it.

2. *We kept Danny informed of any changes in the overall development of Devon's illness.* It was and remains our belief that "updates" are important. One of the difficulties of a sudden death is that it is impossible to have a transition period which helps to bridge the gap between alive and dead. If Devon were going to die, and we always knew that possibility existed even though we initially refused to accept it for her, we wanted Danny to have the chance to "grow" toward that fact rather than to have to deal with a sudden "announcement" of her death. Our updates, therefore, allowed him to better prepare for the ultimate outcome of her illness. Our updates followed the following pattern over a five-month period of time:

(1) "Danny, Devon is sick, and the doctors are trying to find out why."

(2) "Danny, Devon is very ill, but the doctors are going to do everything possible to help her get well."

(3) "Danny, Devon is not doing very well, and there is a chance she won't get well."

(4) "Danny, Devon is just too sick to make it. She has just a little while longer to be with us."

Without some kind of response to her treatment or some kind of miracle, only one last update would be necessary.

3. *We tried to approach Devon's illness in an atmosphere that included closeness, togetherness, love, and care.* After all, we didn't want Danny to fear that we all might leave him.

Children can be very afraid of abandonment. As I look back on our "talks" with Danny, they were usually up in his bedroom, embedded in talk about his day, our family, his friends. We were appropriately concerned about Devon, but Danny's life was of no less importance. Our closeness was expressed by touching, being in the same room together, taking him out to dinner with us. When we were in Los Angeles, we arranged for a loving grandmother and grandfather to stay with him, and we always talked directly to him when we would telephone home.

4. *We tried to share with Danny our real feelings.* Our feelings alternated between hope and anxiety, relief and pain, faith and doubt, understanding and confusion, strength and weakness, peace and anger. It wasn't that we overloaded him with our anxiety, pain, doubt, confusion, and anger; but if we needed to talk about how badly we felt or if we needed to cry, we didn't try to hide these needs. On the other hand, these feelings were balanced with expressions of hope, relief, faith, understanding, strength, and peace. In other words, we tried to be real people, real parents, who were experiencing a situation in which we didn't have all the answers, we weren't always "together." But, we were trying our best to deal with life the best way we knew how.

5. *We found ourselves inviting Danny to share his feelings.* "Danny, I sure feel sad about Devon today. How do you feel?" On the other hand, we didn't try to force him to express himself. As a therapist, I am convinced of the idea that feelings are normal and natural—all of them. It was important to us to let Danny clearly know that his feelings were okay and that it was all right to express them if it would help.

INTERACTING WITH MEDICAL PROFESSIONALS

Another difficult role parents of terminally ill children

are forced to play is that of a mediator between the medical professionals and the ill child. The medical professional is generally intimidating to the lay person. The patient comes to the doctor because the doctor has the knowledge, skill, and experience to make the sick one well. If the sick one knew what to do, the patient wouldn't be asking the doctor how to get well. This situation often creates a superior/inferior dynamic.

In the case of parents, however, they are not necessarily the sick one. Some medical professionals, however, appear to include the family of the sick child as a broader definition of who is the "patient." Any number of times, Carol and I were asked if we would like to see a counseling professional for help. This was done in spite of the fact that we were eventually complimented by Devon's pediatrician that he had always been impressed with the healthy manner in which we had faced her illness.

At one point, a mental health specialist walked into Devon's room and began describing in objective terms "separation anxiety," a disorder children sometimes develop when they are separated from their parents. She never bothered to find out anything about us, nor had she ever visited Devon previously, nor had she deemed it important to ask what my profession was. She assumed we were sick and therefore needed her expertise. After she left the room, we asked each other what that was all about. We never saw her again.

Let me be quick to clarify the fact that I wholeheartedly endorse the idea of a hospital's providing parents with the opportunity to receive counseling from a mental health specialist, be it a psychiatrist, psychologist, family therapist, or clinical social worker. I'm simply saying that medical professionals can prematurely label parents of sick children as a part of their case load and fail to take full advantage of the expertise a parent does bring to the hospital room and the healing process. After all, no one cares as much for the sick child as do the parents.

As Devon's parents, we had been in the constant process of nurturing and caring for her twenty-four hours every day since her birth. We knew her habits, response patterns, and personality. For example, even when Devon was at her worst, no one could get her to eat like Carol could. She knew what Devon would eat, knew the preferred consistencies of food, and all the tricks for getting her to open her mouth! Carol could take one look at the tray of hospital food and immediately know whether Devon would eat it or not.

What is the role of the parent in relation to the medical staff? It is our perception that the doctor was the expert on medical procedure and that we were the experts on Devon. The staff knew the world of the hospital, but we knew Devon's world. The doctor would visit her a couple of times a day for just a few fleeting moments, perhaps to implement a medical procedure; but we would comfort Devon for hours following that procedure. The doctor supported her physical health, and we offered her emotional support.

The radiologist from Los Angeles had only Devon's physical well-being in mind when he suggested we would be taking her to Los Angeles again for radiotherapy. We had much more in mind. We had gone through that process once and knew what it was like to be separated from home, family, and the support of others. Devon, for instance, responded most positively to her brother, Danny. If we had gone to Los Angeles, Danny would not have been able to see her. We also knew that the only way we could continue to comfort Devon through such stress and strain would be for us to receive comfort from our support system at home. And if Devon were to die, wouldn't it be better for all concerned for her to die at home? We thought all of this made great sense.

Unfortunately, the radiologist never realized that our viewpoint was geared to Devon's healing as well. Instead, he interpreted our decision to stay in San Diego as a lack of care for our daughter. Interestingly enough, we were told the next day that if radiotherapy were indicated, the hospital would fund our taking Devon to a private clinic in San Diego. Without our input, however, such a move would never have been contemplated.

Finally, in the end, it was Carol and I who said, "Enough." Devon was dying. It couldn't be denied any longer by us or by the medical staff. Massive dosages of chemicals given at a time when all hope was gone appeared uncaring and inhumane. It would have made her last few days unbearable, and we would have missed that strange comfort that comes when the inevitable is finally accepted.

We will always be grateful for a host of doctors, nurses, technicians, and clerks who for the most part recognized our contribution to Devon's fight for life. At one point, Carol and I felt Devon would be better off if she could stay at home during the day in the comfort and reassurance of her own room. However, we wanted to admit her back into the hospital at night so we could get some much needed rest. We presented the idea to the medical staff. They talked with the admissions office and the formal process of admitting and discharging was waived. We came up with the idea, and the medical staff made it possible.

We learned that the medical professionals and the parents each have a significant, unique, but complementary role to play in the continuing care of a sick child. With mutual respect and care, it is possible for parents to become an integral part of the team.

Many of these professionals, working daily in the arena of life and death, cared deeply for Devon. One registered nurse sent us a card expressing her concern. In addition to the card's verse, she wrote by hand, "I just wanted you to know how much I care."

INTERACTING WITH THE PASTOR

The third special role played by the parents of a terminally ill child involves a unique "dialogue" spoken with the pastor of the family. As Christians, we have heard exhortations that faith in God can help us in times of need. Of course, it is far easier to accept this sermon during those times when life is fairly positive and under control! However, on those occasions when we have heard of another's tragedy, we might have wondered if we could ever have enough faith to withstand the same kind of tragedy if it were to happen to us.

When tragedy does strike, our relationship with the pastor can be one of truly reciprocal support. The pastor comforts us by letting us know that God cares and is in control of our lives and our present circumstances. The pastor's encouragement to stand firm in the midst of overwhelming odds is akin to the nurturing parent who lovingly says to his child, "Come on. I know you can do it!" And you find out that at times, your faith is the only rock left upon which to stand.

How does the parishioner reciprocate? When we can stand firm, retaining our faith with tragedy and despair all around us, the pastor's faith in God is affirmed. All of those sermons were not in vain! A note from our pastor clearly shows the reciprocal nature of the interaction:

> It was a privilege to minister at that precious and personal time, but I can assure you that I was ministered to in a very significant way. I love and appreciate you more than I can say. Your testimony (of faith) has blessed many hearts, including mine. Our prayers continue to be with you.

Both pastor and parishioner rest in the fact that their mutual faith has stood the test of adversity.

In the midst of an ordeal, we are provided the opportunity to experience life to the full. We can hide and grow fearful and bitter, or we can confront our experiences and learn new insights about ourselves and others. One leads to a sense of despair, and the other leads to a sense of integrity.

The Last Flight

*I*s it possible to make every moment count? Is it possible to be aware of the gift of life each day, knowing it will be snatched away at any moment? We tried is all I can say. But the intensity of those days was draining. I promised myself when we brought Devon home that I would not dwell on the end that we knew would come in a few weeks. But the end was with us long before it came, affecting the precious moments that were left and adding poignancy to everyday happenings.

Devon's special joy had been to be outside near flowers. On her first morning home again, the first place we headed was to the patio. The bright sun made checkerboard patterns through the patio cover on the cement below. I placed Devon in a walker. She immediately scooted it over to a blooming plant and pushed her tiny index finger into a blossom and wrinkled up her nose. This was to be a small daily pleasure for her until she grew too weak to move the walker. Then we took a baby swing to the patio so she could still enjoy the outdoor atmosphere of freedom.

There were numerous bike rides through the neighborhood until the bumps in the street or sidewalk made her too uncomfortable. The cancer in her liver seemed to be growing at an alarming rate and made her uncomfortable sitting or reclining. The only evidence of the lungs being affected was a slight cough now and then. I began to wonder if she would make it to her first birthday on July 22, the only one she would ever have. I began to make plans for that day.

I visited a toy store and bought items I thought she could handle easily in bed in a weakened condition: bright colorful fabric blocks, a small cloth doll, and a hand-held music box that she could play by turning a small red handle. Its tune was in a minor key and a bit melancholy, which fit the situation, I thought. As Devon grew weaker and more uncomfortable, her ability to show expression diminished. She became a ghost of the animated, vivacious little girl we knew. It was as if she had given up. Perhaps the last real smile came on her birthday when I held a little cupcake up for her to see and lit the candle. We all sang "Happy Birthday" with our hearts in our throats. She responded with a shadow of a smile and reached for it. We caught the moment forever in a snapshot.

It was a wretchedly sad day, punctuated with thoughtful gifts from friends and family: a matching sundress and bonnet, handmade by a neighbor; a soft little furry toy, just big enough to hold in a small hand; red sandals; and a new dress from the grandmothers. It was almost a relief to all of us when the day was over. It had been like the passing of one last landmark at the end of a long journey.

A few days later my father wrote a letter of encouragement to us. He wrote:

In these difficult days our strength is in the fact that "God is our refuge and strength, a very present help in trouble" (Psalms 46:1). "He shall deliver thee in six troubles; yea in seven there shall no evil touch thee" (Job 5:19). We cannot understand it; we only believe it. So, cast "all your care upon him, for he careth for you" (1 Peter 5:7). In the fiery furnace I think the three Hebrew children were constantly awed by the flames but amazed by the one who voluntarily came to share their expected fate; the result was only a secondary by-product.

The last statement struck a chord of response in me.

I can still see the little uncovered feet bouncing ahead of me as my mother carried Devon into the hospital for the final time. We had kept Devon at home as long as possible. Her discomfort even with medication kept her wakeful during the warm August evenings. Emotionally exhausted during the day and unable to sleep at night, Bill and I found ourselves losing the little strength and control we had left. I contracted one of the worst sinus colds I had ever experienced.

My mother flew out to spend what seemed to be Devon's last days with us. I appreciated not only her nursing care for Devon, but her nurturing support as well. She took over Devon's bathing. It was more than I could stand to look at—the wasted little body and the taut abdomen where the cancer continued to thrive. It eventually became apparent, however, that her surroundings at home were becoming less important. The only time she was comfortable was when she was heavily medicated. Morphine was begun through her i.v. when she was readmitted to the hospital for that final time.

Saturday evening Bill and I sat beside Devon for several hours. We were aware that she had not eaten by mouth for several days. Occasionally she would rouse herself, and I would drop an eye dropper full of water into her parched little mouth. It was like feeding a little bird.

Our pastor, who had not been by for several weeks, dropped by that evening. When he offered a prayer asking for God's will to be done, I found incredibly a little hope left in my heart. I thought, *Even now, Lord, you could touch her.*

It was time to leave and just as we were heading out the door of her room, Bill glanced back.

"Wait, Carol, look at Devon," he said. "She is focusing on you." As I looked back I could see that she had turned her head toward the door and her eyes were following me. During the last several days she had drifted in and out of consciousness under heavy medication. I went back over to the bed and patted her head and kissed her pale cheek. By then her eyes were closed, and I told her good night for the last time.

The call from the hospital came at 6:45 A.M. the following morning. The message was concise: "Devon Rowley's condition is worsening rapidly." The pediatric nurse seemed to be doing her best to maintain her professionalism.

As we hurried to get ready and started down the stairs to the front door, my mother remembers I stopped midway and said, "I want to take a nice blanket." Returning to Devon's nursery I selected a fleecy yellow comforter. I have no memory of it except I remember the yellow blanket was at the hospital later.

Bill commented to my mother as we went out the front door, "Where is the evidence of a heavenly Father's love?"

We ran from the parking lot into the hospital and to the elevator. Hurrying from the elevator to Devon's room, I managed to arrive a few steps ahead of Bill. As I approached the bed, I sensed she was already gone. I laid my hand on her little head and found it still warm. Already her color had changed. I intercepted Bill and told him we were too late. The nurses on duty confirmed she was dead.

We were told that at approximately 6:30 A.M. she was found to have dilated pupils and her heart had begun a slow decline in rate. She had been pronounced dead at 7:00 A.M. just minutes before our arrival. Her last twelve hours in the hospital had been spent essentially dozing; she had been in no obvious distress or discomfort.

That morning as we stood next to her bed, I had the profound sensation that the real Devon wasn't in the room. The little body that had undergone so much pain and illness was now at peace. Curiously, I didn't feel grief in those first few moments. I felt a strong conviction that Devon wasn't present, that she was with God.

A completely spontaneous expression came from Bill's lips the moment he came into the room and saw Devon's body. "We won," he said quietly. It was a statement that wasn't understood fully even by Bill for several years. For the moment, it was a simple statement that finally the cancer had been beaten. For the first time since the diagnosis on April 10, the cancer was not growing. We held each other and let the tears flow as we thought about the great price that had been paid to defeat it—a life gone not long after it had begun.

Devon's pediatrician joined us a few minutes later. He said, "You know, I am aware that you folks have a strong religious faith. I used to have faith, but after seeing this kind of thing happen so often, I have begun to think that if there is Someone in charge up there, there is much evidence of poor administration."

We appreciated his humanity at that moment. Bill responded by telling him that our faith did not exempt us from sickness and death. It was all a part of life. He further shared our belief that God had given us strength throughout the ordeal. We told him of our faith that we would see Devon again.

I handed the yellow blanket to the nurse and asked her to send it with Devon to the mortuary. She told me it wouldn't be necessary. I pressed it into her hands and said, "I know, but I need to think of her covered and cared for a little longer." She squeezed my hand with understanding and took the blanket.

Danny was just finishing his breakfast when we returned home from the hospital. My mother stood nearby as Bill put his arms around Danny and told him that Devon had just died and was with Jesus in heaven. Danny looked at our faces and then down to the floor without crying. He seemed unsure of how he should respond. Bill, sensing this said, "You know, Danny, some people cry when they are sad, like Mom. Some people feel sad in their hearts, but don't cry. Either is all right."

"That's how I am," was all he said. We all hugged each other.

During the days that had preceded Devon's death and in the hours that followed, fragments of a poem had been forming in my mind. Each time I would go over it, adding another line, emotion would sweep over me. Finally I began to put it on paper. When I showed it to Bill, he wanted to use it for her funeral service. "But Carol," he said, "could you put something in the poem about how she loved flowers?" So, I found a way to include a line about flowers.

TO DEVON FROM MOTHER

There was once a bit of sweetness
Borne on the summer air,
Its fragrance filled our lives
And lingered a moment there.

There was once a bit of softness
That caressed us for awhile,
Brown silken curls, big dark eyes,
And a lovely baby smile.

There was once a bit of beauty
That filled our hearts with joy,
A perfect form, a perfect face,
A gift without alloy.

There was once a bit of sunshine
That shone across our days,
A little someone who loved flowers
And gentled us with her ways.

There was once a tiny girl
A little gift from heaven,
A child with beauty soft and sweet,
She was our little Devon

Though now the gift is taken
And the fragrance blooms no more,
Her soft sweet beauty still lives on
In memory's golden store.

As we thought about the memorial service for Devon, we decided to include the giving of flowers to those who came. We knew that the friends and family who came would be there to support us. We also knew that at many such occasions the family who is grieving never comes in touch with the friends attending the service. We would arrange for a large basket of cut carnations to be placed at the door of the chapel. Following the service, we would stand near the door and thank our friends by presenting them with a living memorial of Devon, a flower she would have loved.

I had never realized that people send money as a part of their expression of sympathy. As cards and checks began to come, we talked about how to use the money. Bill remembered the poorly stocked playroom at the Kaiser Hospital where Devon had stayed in San Diego. And we decided to establish a memorial to Devon in which an annual contribution of money or toys is given to the hospital playroom.

Seldom does it rain in San Diego in the summer. Rain is our winter weather. The day before the funeral the skies were cloudy and the humidity so high that you stuck to anything you touched. The house was filled with roses and flower arrangements from many friends. The odor from the flowers, combined with the heavy air, took my breath away.

Bill and I made two painful trips to the memorial park, the first to make arrangements for the service, and the second to view Devon's body. On that second visit, we were shown into a small room filled with flowers and a small white casket. Recorded music droned into my consciousness as we lifted the casket top. A little child, in a christening dress, lay there in front of us. I knew it was Devon's body, but everything seemed so artificial about her. Where was the glowing little girl with the dark lively eyes? This was a little stranger, and it gave me no comfort or sadness to be there looking at her. My immediate reaction was to leave. Bill, on the other hand, thought she looked very natural and beautiful and wanted to spend a few minutes with her body.

The following day it rained a warm tropical mist. I tiptoed into Devon's nursery that day and listened to the rain on the second story roof. It had always been such a comforting sound until now. As I looked around the room at the toys she had touched, her clothes in the closet, I knew I would strip this room bare tomorrow. It would hold only pain for me as it was. It would be a reminder of what might have been. As I went out of the room, I noticed a forgotten plaque on the door. The tape, loosened by the humidity, made it hang limply. It read, "Expect a Miracle." I ripped it from its place and threw it into the wastebasket.

Danny sat beside Bill and me on the first row of the chapel seats. Together we all three focused on the tiny white casket surrounded by flowers in front of us. Bill felt it was best that Danny attend the funeral and be a part of the experience of saying good-by to Devon with us.

I was aware that the chapel had filled up in back of us. Our pastor was speaking in quiet tones. With an inner struggle to keep my emotions in check, I was getting through the service. Then the pastor began to read the poem I had written, and I felt Danny stir and look up at me. I reached over for his hand. What must be going through this little boy's mind? How complete our family had seemed with four members. Now Danny would be an only child again. As the service ended, Bill and I moved to the rear of the chapel where the basket of carnations had been readied. As our friends filed out, we received embraces and words of sympathy. In return, we gave a flower from Devon to each of our friends and thanked them for coming.

The sealing of the crypt followed, with family members standing close by. As we left, I read the bronze plaque on the crypt:

DEVON NICOLE ROWLEY
1976–1977

That beautiful name had been chosen with so much care. In my wildest moments I had never anticipated how it would be to read that name on a tomb. Anguish filled my soul, and blindly I reached out to touch the letters of her name.

Following the funeral, there were many tasks to complete. Relatives to be placed on airplanes, rooms to be emptied of memories, insurance forms to be filed and thank-you notes to be written. They were details for which I felt grateful. But in the middle of any of those tasks, my mind would suddenly remember, and grief would take over. At first, two or three times a day, I would find myself sobbing. It was usually when I was alone in the house. One day I remember Bill's coming in unexpectedly and finding me crying and in anguish. He apologized, said he didn't mean to intrude, and went back outside. We discovered how private grief was. Although we shared as much as we could about the experience, I knew there was nothing I could say to relieve Bill's or Danny's feelings of grief. Likewise, Bill could not reach the depths of mine.

Each day there would be a new batch of sympathy cards. Many were from people we didn't know. Some had also lost a child and heard about us through our friends. Some were to open doors of new friendships later. Other cards were so full of Scripture or platitudes that they preached to me rather than brought comfort. The ones that touched us most were those who simply shared or mirrored our feelings. I remember one in particular from a friend that comforted me greatly. It read, "We grieve with you because we loved her too." Our daughters had been the same age, and they had been together in the church nursery.

As the days passed, the time between the bad times lengthened. Healing was beginning to take place. Like a scab, newly formed, the wound was still very tender and still visible. A picture taken of the three of us a month after Devon died showed all of us smiling. But in each of our eyes was a noticeable lack of positive expression. It was a hurt look. The sensitive camera's eye had uncovered our wound.

Appreciating
the Grief Process

*I*t is normal to grieve. Where, then, did we get the idea that we should be able to overcome the loss of a significant person with ease and dispatch? We all expect and accept sadness and heartache during the days immediately surrounding the funeral, but if we grieve much beyond that, we begin to feel uncomfortable with our inability to handle the death of someone we loved.

Just recently, I had a woman in her sixties visit me for a counseling session. Her forty-two-year-old daughter had died of cancer, and she was suffering greatly from her loss. When she called me on the phone to make her appointment, she said, "I just can't seem to say good-by to her." I got the impression from what she said that her daughter had died about a year earlier; and, therefore, I thought she might need help in resolving her loss.

Again, when she came in for her appointment, I got the distinct impression that her daughter had died many months before. Just to make sure, however, I asked her directly when her daughter had died. I was surprised to learn that her daughter had only been dead for a matter of weeks! Somewhere this woman, like so many of us, had learned that even such a significant loss as losing a child should be resolved quickly and easily. With a great sense of relief, she left my office feeling better about herself and better able to move through the grieving process towards recovery. Her parting words were, "I think I can make it now that I know I'm normal."

There are times when guilt for grieving too long comes from a different source. Rather than being self-imposed, it is relayed in the attitudes and discomfort expressed by others. Perhaps you have been in a group in which the conversation turns to someone who recently lost a parent, a child, a spouse, or a close friend. Someone asks the question, "How is John doing?" The refrain often played back sounds something like, "Oh, he isn't doing very well. I was talking to him the other day and he broke down and cried." The implication is that something is wrong with John. He *should* be doing better. He is grieving too long.

Sometimes others appear to have a strong need for the grieving person to be better. Their need is perhaps not a conscious need and is expressed in a tremendously subtle way. Shortly following Devon's death, I got a call from a friend who asked how I was doing. As honestly as I could, I expressed my feelings of loss, sadness, and despair. In spite of the fact that I gave a comprehensive and full report as to my emotional status, I sensed that my friend did not want to end the conversation. I didn't know why. I found myself repeating earlier statements. Finally, I just happened to say, "But, I'm doing better." In an instant of spontaneity and audible relief, my friend said, "Oh, good! Well, I have to go now. Talk to you later." Slowly, it dawned on me. She couldn't hang up until she knew I was better.

There was someone in our lives, however, who knew better—someone who knew how grief works, someone who gave us "permission" to grieve for as long as was needed. Dr. Keith Olson and his wife, Betty, are special friends of ours, and Keith is a colleague of mine. About a month after Devon died, Keith sat down and wrote us an understanding and insightful one-page letter. It was written by hand and remains in our collection of notes of comfort.

Dear Bill and Carol,

I simply want to give you my greetings and to let you know that Betty and I think of you often. I guess our thoughts are of little value unless they are communicated. We do think of you; we do care about you and pray for you.

Perhaps the several weeks following your loss—after the gathering of relatives and friends—are the loneliest and most difficult. Into this time may I offer encouragement and continuing feelings of concern and support?

Thank you so much for allowing us to be present at Devon's memorial service. Your own memorial of floral remembrances was very touching and warming. I felt a very full two-way flowing of love, compassion, and sadness at the moment you gave to me your gift.

With my love,
Keith

Perhaps it doesn't need to be said, but death is a significant part of the larger life experience described in the professional literature as loss. Is it as comforting to you as it is to me to know that "loss", in turn, is a part of the natural, normal flow of life? In her book *Communication in the Counseling Relationship*, Bonnie Jay Headington speaks of loss as a core experience of life. When we take time to think about it, we have, indeed, been experiencing loss from birth.

As a little boy, my losses were relatively small, but nevertheless significant to me: a few marbles lost in a game played "for keeps," a jacket carelessly left behind on the school playground, a toy forgotten in the empty lot next door.

As I grew older, my losses became even more significant. When I was in about the fourth or fifth grade, my family considered moving from a big two-story Victorian house we had lived in for several years. We found a house that was sufficient for our needs, but we decided not to move. We recognized that we simply didn't want to say good-by to "our old neighborhood." When we finally did move, it wasn't without some trauma that I drove away from the only home I had ever known. Several years later I experienced sincere grief when I visited my childhood neighborhood only to find the old house had been torn down and replaced by a modern office building.

As an adult, my greatest losses are those which center around the loss of relationships with other people. Sometimes it seems to me as though my closest friends always move away just about the time the relationship has developed and matured to a high level of enjoyment, trust, acceptance, and fulfillment.

I'm sure Carol and I will never be able to fully describe the depth of our loss when Devon died. Losing her easily surpasses any loss with which we have had to cope. But it helped me tremendously, and it helps my clients significantly, when they begin to accept loss as a natural part of life, a central experience from birth to death, a fact that has been true since time began. Perhaps the Old Testament book, *Ecclesiastes*, best expresses the ebb and flow of the nature of life:

> There is a time for everything,
> and a season for every activity under heaven:
> a time to be born and a time to die,

a time to plant and a time to uproot,
a time to kill and a time to heal,
a time to tear down and a time to build,
a time to weep and a time to laugh,
a time to mourn and a time to dance, . . .

Ecclesiastes 3:1–4 (NIV)

We hinder healing when we attempt to bypass our time to mourn because we disrupt the natural flow of life.

Psychological studies regarding the nature of loss resulting from death suggest a fairly consistent pattern in terms of what the grief process looks like. But prior to describing the stages or phases of grief, it is helpful to note two ideas that provide insight about what appears to be the "normal" response to death.

The first idea is that loss hurts. Counselor educator Donna Davenport said it simply and clearly when she wrote, "Loss always involves pain." Another writer echoed her thought when he wrote that trauma is always the consequence of loss (Martin Cheikin).

The second idea is that grieving appears to be a natural process for dealing with and eventually healing the pain we experience as a result of our loss of a loved one. In fact, it is only when we accomplish the work of grieving that we resolve our loss.

These ideas give us some important clues as to how we can best recover from the loss of someone we love. We can expect pain, and we can best treat it by giving ourselves permission to grieve. I'm sure it is an uncommon pairing of words for many of us, but Maria Nieto Senour, counselor educator at San Diego State University calls this process "successful grieving." A similar thought is expressed by Donna Davenport when she talks about the "healthy grieving process." I don't know about you, but it helps me to be more patient with myself when the doctor tells me in advance that a shot is going to hurt. I recognize that the pain is a natural consequence of what I have experienced rather than inaccurately concluding that there is something wrong with me because I hurt.

Stages of Grief

Any number of counseling professionals have written about the "stages" of grief (Robert Kavanaugh, Colin Parkes, Elisabeth Kubler-Ross, G.E. Westberg, John Bowlby). In general, the stages include (a) denial; (b) anger and guilt; (c) bargaining; (d) depression; and (e) resolution. Of course, the danger in creating what appears to be separate categories and stages is that it makes it sound like those of us going through grief do so in an orderly manner—in an ever forward-moving process. In reality, however, some individuals may find that the stages overlap somewhat; some may not experience every stage; and others may even experience at times a regression to an earlier stage. Depending on the severity of the loss, these phases can be pronounced or subtle. According to counseling professional Martin Cheikin, "Every loss creates trauma, and different types of loss result in varying degrees of trauma."

A few years after Devon's death, Carol and I had to decide whether or not it would be the humane thing to do to have the local animal shelter end the life of our family pet, a poodle name Suzy. She was an elderly dog, about thirteen years old, and she was suffering from diabetes, losing her sight, her hair, and control of her bladder. We were giving her insulin shots everyday, and we just couldn't seem to bring her diabetes under control. Finally we could not bear her suffering and loss of dignity any longer. I took her to the animal shelter, knowing I would never see her again. As she went with me in complete trust, I was painfully aware of how long she had been with us. She had been a "shower gift" when Carol was pregnant with Danny. She had even gone to Colorado with us when I was working on my doctorate. I cried as I walked out of the shelter and across the parking lot to my car.

I was somewhat surprised, however, to notice that I felt no pain after just a few days. In Devon's case, the pain lasted for a much longer period of time. For several months, I carried such a heavy load that I felt like I was suffocating. I would have to inhale a large breath of air periodically in order to get more oxygen into my lungs. Why the difference? My commitment, investment, identity, and level of care for Devon resulted in greater trauma and pain. The work of grieving was therefore much more visible and difficult.

The stage of *denial* is somewhat perplexing to understand. Death is a fact. Some of us, however, will temporarily deny it. For Carol and me, our denial came as Devon was dying. We tried long and hard to believe she would live. That idea was so central to our belief system that we had to struggle to finally submit to what was reality. Following Devon's death, we could deny it no longer. After all, we had one final "update" to give Danny.

It was slightly different for my mother. Flying to San Diego from her home in San Francisco to attend the funeral, she quietly asked if she could view Devon's body prior to the memorial service. I drove her to the mortuary, and she took one last look at her granddaughter. As we were leaving the memorial park in which the mortuary is located, she turned to me and said, "Thanks, Bill. That will help me with all of this. I just couldn't believe she was dead until I saw her."

Anger was an emotion that both Carol and I felt, but *guilt* was not a part of our experience. At alternating times, we were angry at her disease, the inability of the medical profession to help her, and the silence of God regarding our requests. We never felt guilty, although I have worked with clients who have been angry and/or guilty as a result of losing a child through accidental death. Some have been angry at others who they feel may have carelessly caused the accident, and they have felt guilty because they feel they should have been more watchful as parents. Sometimes a child left behind feels that perhaps he should have died instead and therefore feels guilty. Perhaps the most heart-wrenching sessions I have had with clients are those in which they feel they themselves caused the accident. It is tremendously fulfilling as a therapist to assist these hurting parents, who are both angry at themselves and filled with guilt, by helping them to accept the healing concept that we are all human; that we make, and will continue to make, mistakes; that our intentions as parents are honorable; and that periodically we must forgive ourselves for our fallibility.

Bargaining is generally done before a death occurs. It is a time when many people who are not particularly spiritually oriented return to the faith of their childhood and attempt to bargain with God. "If you will keep our son alive, we will start taking the children to church." Naturally, parents with a strong faith readily turn to God in an attempt to persuade Him to intervene in their child's fight for life.

In an article in *The Personnel and Guidance Journal* (1981), Donna Davenport suggests an interesting idea when she says that loss is difficult for us because we have the illusion that we have control of things. It seems to me that bargaining is consistent with this idea as we only bargain when we believe we have something someone else wants. That means we think we can control the actions of another because we have something he or she values. If we believe God wants a higher level of commitment from us, we can bargain with Him. "I'll give you what you want, but only if You save my son."

Bargaining doesn't always involve a spiritual dimension, however. Carol and I were bargaining, in a sense, when we decided, through our assent to radiotherapy, to go along with the possibility of crippling in order to save Devon's life.

If our efforts to bargain fail, *depression* can be the result. Most of us know what depression feels like, but it can be more intense following the death of someone we loved. As the degree of depression intensifies, we can experience physical symptoms in addition to the depressed mood feeling. We may, for instance, experience temporarily some of the more classical features of clinical depression. In addition to the depressed mood, we may experience a loss of appetite, sleep disturbances, and a loss of energy. We may fatigue quickly, need more rest, and withdraw from people. But in spite of the tendency to withdraw, one way to moderate the depression is to try, within reason, to balance the amount of time spent alone with time spent with people who care. This allows us to "borrow" energy from other people until such time as we can "turn on" our own energy supply.

Finally, we have *resolution*. Patiently allowing yourself to move through the various stages of grief at your own pace enables you to comfortably move away from that which has been lost so that you can reinvest your time and commitment elsewhere. You can therefore begin to place your loss in "memory's golden store" and allow all those pleasurable memories to motivate you to develop new relationships and investments. Resolution leads you to a highly significant insight: It is possible to live without the support of the person you lost.

CHILDREN: COPING WITH GRIEF

Do children manifest the same stages of grief as adults? There is evidence to suggest that the stages of grief are very similar but perhaps much more simplified. For example, in a 1961 issue of the *American Journal of Psychiatry,* John Bowlby indicates only three phases. They are similar to the adult stages of denial, depression, and resolution. He perhaps would include anger in the denial stage.

Recently, I asked my own son, Danny, who is now a freshman in high school, what he remembers about his own experience of grief. At the same time, I recognize the difficulty in trying to recall an event which took place some five years earlier when he was only eight years old. At any rate, Danny told me that he could only recall two stages of grief. First, he remembers being in shock. "I was numb," are his words. That could correlate with the denial stage, which is sometimes accompanied by feelings of shock, or it could be an expression of the depression stage, which can include pain and some disorientation.

Second, Danny remembers coming to a point where he recognized that there was nothing he could do about the situation. His way of saying it today is typical adolescent language, "You have to get on with it." Certainly this is a sign of resolution.

The important thing here is that children do grieve. It may not be a complicated process, but it is a significant step to their own reorganization of life without the lost person. We tried to allow Danny to express his own grief in his own way. He only cried once, and he was relatively self-contained in spite of our making sure he knew he could talk about Devon and share his feelings.

Only once did we have to correct misinformation. Several weeks following Devon's death, Danny asked his mother one day, "Mom, what did Devon look like in the coffin?" Carol explained that she looked pretty much as she always did. "But," he persisted, "what did she look like?" Carol repeated her first response. Finally, he took the direct approach by asking, "Did she just look like bones?" Patiently, Carol decided to try her best to find out why he was struggling with what Devon looked like in the coffin. "Why do you think she would just look like bones?" she asked.

"Well, Grandma said Devon had a beautiful bone structure." Then Carol remembered that my mother, upon her return from viewing Devon's body at the mortuary, had remarked about her beauty. In doing so, she had said, "Carol, Devon had such a beautiful bone structure."

A little boy, only eight years old, trying desperately to figure everything out, concluded from his grandmother's remark that only his sister's skeleton was in the coffin. We were instantly grateful for the fact that Danny felt free to ask his mother about something that was confusing him. We will probably never know exactly our own impact on Danny's healing process; we only know that he has resolved the issue for now in a manner satisfactory to him.

I often hear from clients the question, "How long will it take me to get over this?" The depth of pain and the duration of grief is closely related to the value you place on that which is lost. When it was advisable to take our dog to the animal shelter, I grieved for several days. When I felt the loss of Devon, I experienced grief to one degree or another for a number of months. The pain gradually decreases, however, as one moves further and further beyond the immediacy of the loss and as investments are made in other people and activities. Periodically, many grieving people experience something that pricks a memory and the pain returns. However, these "islands of sorrow," as counseling professional Charles Heikkinen described them in an article in the 1979 issue of *The Personnel and Guidance Journal,* grow further and further apart.

There is a time to mourn. But this time of grieving can be a positive experience. After all, it is a healthy, normal process. There is a pattern of grieving in which we all share, even though we each experience loss in a unique and individual way. The process, if allowed and respected, leads to recovery.

When we are in the middle of the process, we sometimes wonder if we will ever live through it. One of my clients who had lost a small child of his own asked me one day, "Will I ever be able to remember him without the pain?" Yes. The end does come, and it leads to healing.

Part Three

THE
END

Prevailing Calm

As we looked back on the events which compounded what could be called a tragedy, we found that much of our frustration and grief centered around events that were completely beyond our control. As Devon's condition deteriorated, it was agonizingly frustrating to be able to do nothing.

During the weeks and months that followed her death, however, it became apparent that we once again had something under our control—our response to tragedy. And, although we had a mixed bag of emotions with which to deal as a part of that response—anger, grief, relief, and depression, to name a few—we also had a need to create something meaningful and positive out of what seemed a meaningless waste of a beautiful life.

Bill's idea of creating a memorial at the hospital seemed a positive gesture. We contacted the hospital administrator.

He turned out to be a friend from college days. The wheels were set in motion, and by Christmas 1977, a plaque had been placed on the door of the Children's Playroom at the Kaiser Hospital in San Diego. It read:

> The toys and equipment in this room
> have been donated in loving memory
> of Devon Nicole Rowley.

A large, closed closet was built to store new games and toys, replacing an old toy box. Small tables and chairs, a play stove and other equipment followed. An external gesture seemed a practical focus for building a positive response.

I would be less than honest, though, if I did not share that there were moments when the resolve to have a positive response to tragedy failed. One path that never ceased to lead to a negative end was what I will call the "whys." As parents with a strong Christian faith, it was only natural that some of my questions centered around our confusion regarding what appeared to be God's failure to intervene in our ordeal. "Why did we as Christians have to experience such a loss? Were we being punished? Were we being censored as parents? Why? Why?"

I think Bill's practicality helped me as much as anything else in this particular situation. His explanation to Devon's pediatrician as to how we were able to maintain a faith seemed to fit this "Why?" Bill admitted that if he thought God had singled us out or in some way zapped us, he would be unable to handle the whole thing. Believing that instead we were just experiencing a part of life, which happens to include sickness and death, made sense to him and helped me as well.

Another "Why?" that was answered to my satisfaction came through a letter from my mother. I had expressed the thought that I sometimes wondered why Devon had been born at all when she was here for such a short time and had suffered so much. My mother, in an expression of her faith, wrote that she was thankful Devon had been born so that we might be able to enjoy her company for eternity. That brought immediate comfort.

One Sunday at church I encountered a friend of ours who also brought comfort through an exciting new thought of transcending time. She expressed the view that as people we are so limited to a past, present, and future time perspective. In God's eyes, time has no such dimensions or limits. Therefore, it might be possible that Bill and I could be experiencing Devon in heaven now by transcending time. I reasoned that indeed if Devon was experiencing her first day of eternity, which would last forever, it could also include my first day as well. It seemed that God was bringing others to me with comfort that contributed to my positive response, even when it faltered along the way.

He was also making the Bible come alive for me. One afternoon I was visited by two neighbors who brought a beautiful basket of fruit. As we talked, one made the comment that she had observed strong people were often required to endure tragedies like we had been through recently. I did my very best to correct her assumption. I told her that we were not strong and had not felt strong while going throught the experience. I told her our faith in God had held us steady. I kept thinking of all the tears that had been shed along the way, tears that could erupt even now at the most unexpected times, over some sweet memory of little Devon. No, we had been only very human.

Not long after that conversation with my neighbors, I was reading 2 Corinthians 4:7–9 in the New Testament. It read:

> But this precious treasure—this light and power that now shine within us—is held in a perishable container, that is, our weak bodies. Everyone can see that the glorious power within must be from God and is not our own. We are pressed

on every side by troubles, but not crushed and broken. We are perplexed because we don't know why things happen as they do, but we don't give up and quit. We are hunted down but God never abandons us. We get knocked down, but we get up again and keep going (TLB).

What may have appeared to others as our strength had been God's strength in us. How many times I had prayed for His assurance during the whole experience—never grasping that He *was* our strength and entered into the experience with us. It hadn't been necessary for Him to send assurance. He had become our means of survival from within. I'm sorry I saw it most clearly in retrospect.

Within a week of Devon's funeral, when I was still feeling very fragile, I received a call from a woman who had gone through the library program at San Diego State University with me. She told me of an opening in a nearby school district for elementary librarians. She asked if I might be interested. Somehow I hated telling her, but I explained what we had just gone through. She apologized, and I remember telling her I would consider applying for the job. But inwardly, I was convinced that the timing was all wrong. Maybe in six months, when I didn't think of Devon constantly, I would be ready to work. I knew that school started in less than a month. I felt too fragile emotionally for any challenge like a new job.

Imagine my surprise when Bill expressed enthusiasm for the idea. He said, "When you're ready, there may not be a job waiting." Realizing how true that was and how few openings there seemed to be in my new field, I began to consider the dim possibility of working. Perhaps God was providing a positive way for me to join the world again. How ironic that God should provide for my emotional needs when He had not provided for Devon's physical needs. I let the thought hang unresolved.

The appointment to interview for the position was arranged. The morning came and I dressed nervously. Bill sensed my uncertainty and my fear of trying to make a favorable impression. What he told me that morning I have repeated to myself on other intimidating occasions: "Carol, you never need to be afraid of life and people again. After all, you have faced one of the worst experiences life has to offer, the death of your child, and you survived."

Three weeks later I found myself in an elementary school library, introducing children's literature to grade schoolers. I am convinced that taking the job helped me move into a new chapter of life in a positive way.

It isn't possible to make every moment count. To do so would make life too poignant to be enjoyed. So there are many wasted moments—many things left unsaid or deeds undone. But that is the luxury of life and good health. However, as the months passed following Devon's death, we noticed small changes in our lifestyle. And I felt that we were "making the most of the moment" a bit more often now. We had always been planners—nothing much was left to chance. But now a sense of spontaneity seemed to invade us once in a while. We took three major trips: one to Colorado for Christmas, one to Washington, D.C., in the spring, and one to Hawaii in July. There was a sense of "Why wait? There is no certainty of next year or years to come. Let's do it now."

Bill had always been financially conservative. But the Christmas following Devon's death, he bought me a diamond ring. When he presented it to me, there was a little card attached that said, "This is in memory of Devon and in celebration of our lasting love."

Danny's fourth grade year seemed to go well. He had been placed in a class for the gifted after being tested the spring before. Among his new and interesting learning experiences was an activity that involved making a notebook of feelings. Each page in the notebook began with a certain feeling and was then followed by the child's response, including the drawing of a picture. As I looked through it, I was impressed by the honesty and simplicity Danny expressed. Then I came to the page for "sad feelings." Tears filled my eyes as I read Danny's words: "Sad is when someone you love dies." There in the center of the page was a small white casket that he had drawn with flowers nearby. I knew Danny was working out his feelings of loss, as were Bill and I.

One evening a few days later, Danny came into the kitchen while I was fixing dinner and handed me a card he had found tucked under the couch. He was crying as he handed it to me. "I had almost forgotten her," he said, "and then I found this." It was a birthday card to "Sister" that he had signed and given her on her one and only birthday. I realized that she was still very much a part of us, sometimes more vividly than others.

Each New Year's Eve our church has a service from 11:00 P.M. until a little after midnight. As part of the service, a few members are asked to share in a reflective manner an experience, positive or negative, from the past year. New Year's Eve of 1977, Bill was asked to reflect on our experience of Devon's illness and death. His mother had come down to join us for the holidays and attended the service with us.

The church looked beautiful that night in the blaze of candlelight and greenery. When Bill began his brief reflection of our tragedy and God's provision of strength, I felt a growing sense of God's presence. There was an unexplainable sense of assurance. A thought invaded my mind: *See, I was there with you through it all.* It was as real as if someone had spoken audibly. It was the first time since the trauma had begun that I felt my faith was rewarded by a sense of overwhelming peace and healing.

After the service, I turned to Bill's mother to see if she, too, had experienced the same reassurance. Her comment

was, "No, it was like going to another funeral service to
hear Bill tell about the experience again." I realized, then,
that God had personalized His message of peace to me. I
hoped Bill's mother would soon find a sense of peace herself. I knew how hard Devon's death had been on her. Devon had been her youngest grandchild, a bookend after
one older granddaughter and four grandsons.

A further reassurance came one Sunday not long after
that as I sat listening to a sermon on Jesus in Gethsemane.
I remembered my own Gethsemane, the night in prayer
following the announcement of Devon's status as a terminal
cancer patient. I realized that Jesus had made a request in
the Garden. Like mine, it had not been answered. Perhaps
the enormity of His situation had weighed on Him to the
point of His requesting the Father to "let the cup pass."
Then the thought followed: *God Himself surely understood my
loss completely, having watched a beloved Son suffer and die.*
How it comforted me to know I had a heavenly Father who
knew so much more about loss and love than I would ever
know or experience.

Bill, too, was finding comfort and new meaning in his
life. Capable, articulate, and one who exudes confidence,
Bill has always been one who appears to have it all together.
To others he always looks as if he has things under control.
For this reason he easily earns the respect and admiration
of those around him—and the reputation of "good ole
dependable Bill." For years as guidance coordinator at San
Diego County Department of Education, Bill had only revealed his strengths and, for the most part, received only
respect. And, although respect feels good and is important,
it doesn't seem to unlock much in the way of love from
others.

When Devon died there was something else for Bill to
share—a new vulnerable spot which included a lot of pain
and human struggle. Bill soon found that when he had an

opportunity to share his vulnerabilities, he was rewarded with feelings of warmth and love from those around him. They in turn opened themselves to him. However, many of Bill's colleagues didn't always know how to approach him on his loss, and many assumed he would not wish to discuss it.

Two experiences, both professional meetings, allowed Bill the opportunity to enjoy a warmer relationship with his colleagues. In 1977, Bill was elected president of the California Personnel and Guidance Association. Each year the presidents of the state associations from the thirteen western states gather for a conference to share issues and ideas of importance in the field of counseling. In a smaller subgroup in which he was participating, Bill and his colleagues were attempting to identify a human rights issue that could be supported by counselors in all thirteen states.

Later Bill told me that he shared with the group his experience of losing Devon. He told them that while Devon was living, there had been questions from his colleagues as to her condition or how the family was doing. But following her death and the traditional gestures of sending flowers or cards or money, all communication had stopped. He explained how his peers had assumed that all trauma was over and there was nothing to discuss. He suggested that perhaps they thought it would be too painful for him to speak about the loss. But Bill went on to explain that for him the experience had been far from over. He had just begun a grieving process that would take months to complete. He told the group that he needed to share thoughts about the experience with other professionals in his field, explaining how he had observed that it was both painful and pleasurable to talk about Devon: painful because once again the loss was underlined, but pleasurable because it brought her back for a moment in conversation.

As Bill finished his remarks, he noticed how quiet the room was and that several were brushing away tears. Then, as though someone had primed a pump, various people began to share their experiences of loss—loss through divorce, loss of community through relocation, and loss through the death of a loved one. The meeting concluded with the establishment of a project to increase the knowledge and skill level of counselors in the thirteen western states so that they would be able to counsel more effectively clients who had experienced loss.

One of the goals of the project was to attempt to get the national association, the American Personnel and Guidance Association, to publish a special issue on loss in its official publication, *The Personnel and Guidance Journal.* In February, 1981, the issue was published and sent to approximately 40,000 counseling professionals across the United States.

Another opportunity for Bill to share his loss experience arose unexpectedly at the California Personnel and Guidance Association's convention held in San Diego in 1981. Max Lerner, the noted columnist for the New York *Post,* had been invited to be one of the speakers at the convention. A few days before his scheduled arrival, he became very ill and had to cancel his trip. Rather than cancel the session at which he would have spoken, Bill, as a past president of the association, was asked to address the conventioneers.

Proposition 13, a tax-cutting initiative, had recently been approved by California voters. The morale of counselors in schools and other public agencies throughout the state was particularly low because of the impending loss of many jobs in the field. So Bill, even though he had suffered a different kind of loss, decided to share his own therapeutic process in dealing with loss.

Although he did not make a religious presentation, he based his speech on some thoughts from John Claypool's book, *Tracks of a Fellow Struggler.* Claypool had lost a daughter to cancer and had a comforting interpretation of Isaiah 40:31.

> They shall mount up with wings as eagles;
> they shall run, and not be weary; and they
> shall walk, and not faint (KJV).

Bill shared with the group his personal loss of a daughter. He described his own grieving process as "walking, but not fainting." When he talked of how he began to resolve her loss, he described himself as being able to "run again, and not grow weary." Finally, when he grasped the idea that Devon had been healed in death (if being free from disease and pain constitutes healing), he described himself as being able to "soar on wings of eagles."

Several people came up to Bill following the session and shared with him how meaningful his presentation had been. Although they had told no one else, they were either experiencing loss or were about to go through a similar experience with a loved one. Once again, Bill discovered how much we touch others when we dare to share ourselves.

Now as a full-time therapist in private practice, he finds his own loss often helps him relate to those whose loss and difficulties in life have brought them to a counseling center and to him.

A few years ago, Bill decided this concept of sharing vulnerabilities had a place within the Christian community and he decided to teach an adult Sunday school class at our church. Since then he has been sharing his life with others and learning what it means to enter into the struggles of others who are fellow Christians. The focus of his class has been not only on the struggle, but on the overcomer, Jesus Christ, who walks the path with us and brings joy in the midst of the struggle.

If there could have been a medical solution for Devon's cancer, it most certainly would have glorified God. And the world could have profited by such an uplifting experience. On the other hand, if God would have chosen a miraculous healing for Devon and restored her to us, that would also have been something the world would have heard about. Either option I felt was appropriate. From the Christian perspective, though, both would have been a temporary answer as she would have experienced death at some time in her life. The healing He chose to bring her, although not my idea, was a divine answer lasting for eternity. I find great comfort in Isaiah 25:8 which says, "He will swallow up death [the cancer] in victory [eternal life]; and the Lord God will wipe away tears from off all faces" (KJV).

God's answer was certainly not the option we were open to receive. But like ripples on a pond when something is dropped on the surface, Devon's life and death disturbed the calm of our life. And those ripples continue to move outward bringing new circles of meaning to us.

I agree with what Anne Morrow Lindbergh says, in her book *Hour of Gold, Hour of Lead:*

> I do not believe that sheer suffering teaches. If suffering alone taught, all the world would be wise, since everyone suffers. To suffering must be added mourning, understanding, patience, love, openness, and the willingness to remain vulnerable.

Bill and I are willing to remain open and vulnerable because we have found that to experience loss is to find new meaning in life.

Experiencing
Recovery

I have always enjoyed time spent in the lost and found department of an elementary school. In one of Danny's schools, the "department" was contained in a big round barrel. It was full and overflowing with lost items such as jackets, purses, belts, hats, along with other articles of clothing. I can't remember what Danny had lost, but the school secretary led me back through a hall and into a room where a collection of items had been stored. There it was, this great big barrel.

I was surprised to experience a rush of anticipation as I began to sift and sort through the unclaimed treasures. Had the experience tapped a long lost memory of looking through a similar barrel when I was but a little boy? Perhaps. But I believe the reason lies elsewhere. I think there is no other experience in life which brings such immediate relief as when you find something which is lost. An umbrella, a set of keys, your wallet, self-esteem, self-identity, a child.

We lost Danny once in a Sears store. Like many small children who go shopping with their parents, he was "here" and then not "here." Can't you hear the desperate refrain of all parents? "But he was just *here* a second ago! Where did he go?" We found Danny in an aisle by himself, with big frightened eyes and a sense of panic rising to the surface.

You could see an almost instant look of relief capture his face when we found him. I'm familiar with the theories that suggest that abandonment is one of the greatest fears children have. However, sometimes I wonder, if in a child's mind, his parents are lost and he finds them! No matter which is true, it is certainly a relief to find that which is lost.

Perhaps part of the reason despair is so great when loved ones are lost through death is that one has the sense that they are "gone." One of my colleagues, in his own attempt to understand just what had happened when Devon died, said to me, "Bill, the tragedy of this whole thing is that you have been deprived of an intimate relationship with someone you loved." For a year I thought he was absolutely right, and he *was* in one sense. But in a comforting moment, I discovered that he wasn't entirely right at all.

It is true that sometimes while rummaging through a barrel or box of lost items, we find what we lost. During those periodic searches, however, I learned something of note. When looking for one item, you sometimes find another that you didn't know was lost. Or, more likely, you find an item you knew you had misplaced but had long ago given up on ever finding it. The consequent relief, or joy, is every bit as pleasurable, and it may even be greater because, in despair, you had given up all hope.

We often look for hope during the beginning stages of a traumatic experience in a different place than we do during the healing stages of overcoming tragedy. And although hope is a reasonable expectation, its source can be surprising and unexpected. Similar to looking through a barrel of lost articles, it is possible to suffer the loss of a loved one and in our desperation, find something else of great value. How can a mother and father even entertain such a thought? It was only near the end of our journey that we discovered the answer.

It is an exciting thought to consider that the darkest hours of tragedy can become the seedbed for a higher level of self-awareness, understanding, and maturity. Counselors often find that clients who suffer from significant loss experience positive personality growth when they successfully grieve and resolve their loss. According to Charles Heikkinin, "Counseling for loss, therefore, aims not merely at acceptance but also at overall personality growth." Much of this personality growth stems from new perceptions and assumptions never before held or considered by the client prior to the loss.

Maria Nieto Senour, in the February 1981 issue of *The Personnel and Guidance Journal*, notes that clients often become aware of a strength and resiliency previously unknown to them.

In my own counseling practice, I have found that my clients who have suffered significant loss and have recovered from its devastating effects are better able to (a) accept and experience loss as an integral part of life, (b) appreciate those relationships and circumstances of current value and import, (c) take risks and make new commitments, and (d) deal with changes in life.

It is only the obvious to suggest that each person who experiences loss will learn unique lessons from the experience. Perhaps it would be helpful, however, to share with you what Carol and I have "found" as a result of our loss of Devon.

First, we found a new appreciation and love for each other. I was impressed with Carol's strength, her ability to "take over" when my energy was depleted during Devon's illness and following her death. Carol, on the other hand, experienced my vulnerability, my need to sometimes lean on her in the midst of overwhelming tragedy. We learned we could respond honestly to each other in relationship to the other's current state. We shared, therefore, each other's strength.

In an earlier chapter, I shared the idea that parents of terminally ill children can really benefit from each other if they are not required to play a "set role" with each other: the husband always playing the strong role and the wife always responding as the weaker one. Such a dynamic can have devastating consequences. For example, the percentage of couples who have experienced the loss of a child and who divorce some time following the death of the child is alarmingly high.

It is my opinion that couples who have set roles increase the chances of growing distant and potentially losing their marriage. The loss of a child is devastating in and of itself. If the roles in the marriage are too rigid, it is impossible for the "strong" partner, whether husband or wife, to provide enough strength for both. The "strong one" is overwhelmed by the task and begins to pull away, and the "weak one" is disappointed by the other's inability to make things better and withdraws. Such increasing distance means that each bears the pain of their loss alone. A wall has been built, shared intimacy has been damaged, and separation results. Divorce may eventually follow.

Carol and I will forever be grateful that Devon's death had the opposite result on our relationship. Our response to each other was deepened rather than distanced. Our effort to jointly write Devon's story is but one expression of our sharing our loss together rather than alone.

Second, we found our faith in God to be strong and valid. Have you ever thought that you would be unable to withstand a particular tragedy if it happened to you? Both Carol and I had experienced similar thoughts, but we found that our faith not only withstood the worst test we could possibly arrange, but it is stronger today than it was prior to Devon's loss.

How can that possibly happen? Robert Kavanaugh in his book *Facing Death* suggests that persons who have faced death must ventilate their feelings, say good-by to the person who was lost, and let go. In other words, it is only as we let go that we even have the capability for new insight, new commitments, new relationships that take the place of the old.

Let me share an example of a new insight I learned after I let go of Devon. My initial understanding of "cure" and "healing" was rather narrow and conventional: Devon's doctor would treat her medically, continue telling us that she was responding nicely to the treatment, report that her x-rays showed no sign of cancer, and at the end of five years, pronounce her cured. The option, of course, would be for her doctor to announce that she somehow had been miraculously cured. To such an event, we would have attributed her healing as an answer to our many prayers. But, Devon died.

I remember so vividly my first remark upon seeing Devon just minutes after her death. It was spontaneous and without prior thought. It was, "We won." It is true that I did not completely understand that statement although on the surface it related to the obvious: If Devon were dead, the cancer could not be growing any longer. In that sense, we had won.

Three years following Devon's death, however, I began to understand that remark which had come from deep within me. Essentially, I formulated a broader-based concept of what healing means, one which could include my experience with Devon and yet be consistent with my principles of faith. Being healthy is the opposite of being ill. If one is ill, healing is what must happen in order for illness to cease and health to return. The moment life left Devon, she no longer suffered any disease, pain, or discomfort. In my mind, necessarily stretched by Devon's death, I let go of the idea that healing is synonymous with living. Devon was well, and without disease or pain, but she was not living with me any longer.

In treating cancer, there are three medically accepted procedures for treatment: surgery, chemotherapy, and radiotherapy. Devon had all three. None of these treatments ended her disease. Only death brought release and relief from cancer. I have come to believe that death can be perceived as a treatment which brings healing. I would have preferred that any of the other treatments would have been successful. And I still do. Thankfully, many children respond positively to these three medically accepted treatment modes. Regardless, Devon is no longer in pain.

Now let me quickly state that I am not making a case for euthanasia, an act of allowing someone who is hopelessly sick or injured to die. Carol and I tried every way possible within the limits of accepted medical practice to bring about healing for Devon. Right up to a few days from the end, she was treated with massive doses of chemotherapy, and she remained under the care of the medical staff in a hospital until the moment she died—all without any positive results. It was only when she died naturally that she was released from her ordeal. In my mind, she was healed and is free from disease and suffering.

Carol and I prayed for healing. Initially, we believed she wasn't healed because she had died. Could it be that we had the strategy for healing confused with the end result of healing?

Perhaps to some I have been laboring to justify my faith in light of Devon's death. To the contrary, I believe that our understanding of our experiences and circumstances is often limited to our inexperience, our narrow view of life, and the lessons we have learned previously.

Jean Piaget, a Swiss psychologist, was the world's foremost authority on what is called in psychological circles *intellectual development*. In other words, he tried to grasp through research just how the mind develops. Robert Biehler, one of many teachers who have attempted to explain the complex theories of Piaget, describes two important concepts of the developing intellect. The concepts are assimilation and accommodation. Oversimplified, *assimilation* is that process by which we fit into our existing structure of intellect any new experience we might have. Assimilation may mean that the new experience fits easily, or it may mean that the existing intellect might have to be expanded a bit to include it. For example, assimilation took place with the expansion of my understanding of healing, a concept I already knew about. *Accommodation,* however, is necessary when the novel experience does not fit anywhere in our existing understanding of life, and we must therefore make room for it. I had to accommodate the knowledge that it is possible to discover something of great value as a consequence of significant loss.

I do not know how much of my faith will be "expanded" as a result of our experience with Devon. But recently (five years following her death) I realized that all the time that we prayed for Devon's healing, I had not thought of praying for mine. Certainly I did not experience physical pain, but the possibility of emotional scarring was very real. It was extremely comforting to me, however, to realize that not only was Devon healed, but I have been healed from the emotional pain of her tragedy, even though I did not specifically ask for it. Immediately my mind grasped the verses in Ephesians 3:20–21 of the New Testament:

> Now to him [Jesus Christ] who is able to do immeasurably more than we ask or imagine [think], according to his power that is at work within us, to him be glory in the church and in Christ Jesus throughout all generations, for ever and ever! Amen (NIV).

The third insight we have found as a result of our loss centers around the idea that Devon continues to be a meaningful part of our lives in spite of her death. The colleague that I mentioned earlier felt as though we had lost our capacity to share an intimate relationship with Devon. We have found that to be true in the usual sense, but completely erroneous in another.

Several months ago, Carol and I were driving to church on a Sunday morning. Danny was not with us because he had gone to a youth camp for the weekend. Forgetting he was gone, I turned to say something to him, thinking he was in the rear seat of the car. Of course, he wasn't there. I suddenly missed him as I was incapable of experiencing him unless he was physically present.

In Devon's case, I experience her anytime! I am not limited to her physical presence. No, I don't see visions of her, and I don't hear voices. I do, though, remember all of the good times (I have wonderful memories), I experience pleasure in how much I love her, and I appreciate the continuing positive impact she has made upon my life.

I related this fact to a friend of mine one day, a successful child psychiatrist in San Diego. He quickly explained, "Why, you have internalized her. She's a part of you!" What an absolutely astounding discovery. Carol and I didn't "lose" her after all. She is an integral part of us. We will experience and know her forever.

Fourth, we have found that the loss of a child can lead to significant personal growth. In my own case, Devon, just a little girl who lived with us for thirteen months, is responsible for a dynamically changed pattern in which I relate to other people. Carol has already outlined the idea that I have tried to share my vulnerabilities with others within a context of strength. Previously, I had pretty much shared only my strength, competence, and control.

About one year following Devon's death, I had an opportunity to enter a therapeutic relationship with another professional. Only this time, I was the client. I remember describing my family to my therapist. When I got to Devon I said, "The thing I liked most about her was her softness. I really valued that." Since that moment, I have attempted to express a very real part of me that had been repressed for a long, long time: my vulnerability. I learned from Devon of my need for the love of people around me, and I had never let that be known before. I'm sure I have a long way to go in allowing other people to see the real, inside me. Psychologists, particularly Sidney Jourard, call this the transparent self. But every once in a while, I receive real encouragement that I am on the right track. One such experience occurred about a year ago. I was invited to present a workshop for counselors in Idaho. One of the conference participants was Dale Schmaljohn, an old friend of mine. We had met at the University of Northern Colorado several years before. He knew me as an intense, anxious, competitive doctoral student!

Dale had called me long distance in San Diego when he learned that I was coming to Idaho. He invited me to spend the night in his home in Boise on the night prior to our driving to McCall the next morning. We would be able to catch up on old times and mutual friends. We had only been up about an hour the next morning when Dale turned to me and spontaneously said, "Bill, you've changed." I asked what he meant as the statement took me by surprise. He said, "You're more relaxed, kind of mellow."

It was then that I remembered my description of Devon: "The thing I liked about her was her softness. I really valued that." A friend had sensed Devon's softness in me. I can only say that I am grateful that she has influenced my life in such a sensitive way, and I appreciate a friend who was able to sense it.

Fifth, we have found that we are much better able to respond to the continuing difficulties of life. In Tracks of a Fellow Struggler,

John Claypool wrote, "The patterns we develop early in relation to our 'little griefs' will affect how we react when the trauma of bereavement comes upon us" (p. 87). We have also found the reverse to be true. Our efforts to respond in a positive manner to our bereavement have enhanced our ability to respond to the daily trials of life.

After all, we grieved over the loss of our daughter, Devon, but in the end we found healing.

Epilogue

July 22, 1982. Devon would have been six years old today. She would have been tall for her age, her eyes large and dark like her father's.

As I think about the party that might have taken place today, the sound of little girls together, I find there is no pain in the thought—only a sense of regret for a relationship that was cut short. However, there is not a day that goes by that Devon doesn't cross my mind. She is in my soul.

And even though the last five years have brought healing for the open wound of loss, sometimes at the sight of another dark-eyed girl, a quick memory of little Devon leaves a catch in my throat. But the child receives a smile that is given in Devon's memory, and the moment passes without pain. Sometimes Devon is remembered when little girls go by on their way to school, swinging their lunch pails. (She would have started first grade this fall.)

Through her coming and her abrupt departure, we have come to know better a Savior who walks through the valley of the shadow of death, as well as on the pathways of sunshine.

We understand that life has no guarantees when you are a Christian. Except there is Someone who will never leave you, nor forsake you in life's situations if you belong to Him.

A bright pot of flowers on the patio conjures a picture of a tiny nose poised to smell and a little finger extended to point out a blossom. I feel a quickening of anticipation for the first day in heaven, for I know a little girl will meet me there, and we will spend eternity's first day together. A foolish request comes to mind and forms a prayer on my lips: "Lord, give Devon a kiss for me and wish her Happy Birthday."

Bibliography

Biehler, Robert F. *Psychology Applied to Teaching*. Boston: Houghton Mifflin Company, 1974.

Bowlby, John. *Attachment and Loss: Separation*. New York: Basic Books, 1973.

Bowlby, John. "The Adolf Meyer Lecture: Childhood Mourning and Its Implications for Psychiatry." *American Journal of Psychiatry*, 1961, 118, 481–498.

Cheikin, Martin L. "Loss and Reality." *The Personnel and Guidance Journal*, 1981, 59, 335–338.

Claypool, John. *Tracks of a Fellow Struggler*. Waco, TX: Word Books, 1974.

Davenport, Donna S. "A Closer Look at the 'Healthy' Grieving Process." *The Personnel and Guidance Journal*, 1981, 59, 332–335.

Erikson, Erik H. *Identity: Youth and Crisis*. New York: W. W. Norton Company, 1968.

Headington, Bonnie Jay. *Communication in the Counseling Relationship.* Cranston, RI: The Carroll Press, 1979.

Heikkinen, Charles A. "Counseling for Personal Loss." *The Personnel and Guidance Journal,* 1979, 58, 46–49.

Johnson, Clarence D. (Ed.). "Change: A Model for Counseling in the Future." *Guidance Personnel 1984: Models for the Future,* California Personnel and Guidance Association Monograph Number 11, 1976, 1–7.

Jourard, Sidney, M. *The Transparent Self.* New York: D. Van Nostrand Company, 1971.

Kavanaugh, Robert E. *Facing Death.* Baltimore: Penguin Books, 1974.

Kubler-Ross, Elisabeth. *On Death and Dying.* New York: Macmillan, 1969.

Kushner, Harold, S. *When Bad Things Happen to Good People.* New York: Schocken Books, 1981.

Lindbergh, Anne Morrow. *Hour of Gold, Hour of Lead.* New York: Harcourt, Brace, Jovanovich, 1973.

Marshall, Catherine. *Adventures in Prayer.* Lincoln, VA: Chosen Books, (distrib. by Fleming H. Revell, Old Tappen, NJ), 1975.

Maslow, Abraham H. *Motivation and Personality.* New York: Harper, 1954.

Parkes, Colin M. *Bereavement Studies of Grief in Adult Life.* New York: International Universities Press, 1972.

Parkes, Colin M. "The First Year of Bereavement." *Psychiatry,* 1970, 33, 444–467.

Peck, M. Scott. *The Road Less Traveled.* New York: Simon and Schuster, 1978.

Purkiser, W. T. *When You Get to the End of Yourself.* Grand Rapids, MI: Baker Book House, 1973.

Rickman, J. (Ed.). *A General Selection from the Works of Sigmund Freud,* Garden City, New York: Doubleday Anchor, 1957.

Rowley, Carol A. *The Effects of Bibliotherapy on Elementary*

Students' Self-Concepts. Unpublished master's thesis, San Diego State University, 1977.

Schaeffer, Edith. *Affliction.* Old Tappan, New Jersey: Fleming H. Revell Company, 1978.

Senour, Maria Nieto. "Project Loss: Sensitizing Ourselves to Grief." *The Personnel and Guidance Journal,* 1981, 59 389–392.

Shostrom, Everett L. *Manual for the Personal Orientation Inventory.* San Diego, California: Educational and Industrial Testing Service, 1966.

Silverman, Robert E. *Psychology* (Brief Edition). New York: Appleton-Century-Crofts, 1971.

Westberg, G. E. *Good Grief.* Philadelphia: Fortress Press, 1962.